Why Is John Lennon Wearing A Skirt?
and other stand-up theatre plays

Adult Child/Dead Child
'A strangely exhilarating experience as well as a subtle exploration of a personality under siege.' *Time Out*

Why Is John Lennon Wearing A Skirt?
'In many ways Ms Dowie is the female counterpart to Quentin Crisp. Her rejection of femininity is as uncompromising as his effeminacy and equally unacceptable to radicals as to conservatives.' *Evening Standard*

Death and Dancing
'A fast, furious and often uncomfortable exploration of sexuality and gender . . . She makes you laugh as she kicks you in the teeth.' *Guardian*

Drag Act
'A short, sharp, illustrated monologue which shows that the politically correct psycho-babble of gay culture is every bit as suffocating as any other.' *Sunday Times*

Leaking From Every Orifice
'This very funny show is not solely Dowie's inimitable account of the crappiness of being Mum; it's also probably the most unusual revenge comedy ever staged.' *What's On*

Claire Dowie is a writer/performer/poet/comedian and pioneer of what she calls 'stand-up theatre'. She started out writing and performing poetry on the original so-called 'alternative' comedy circuit in London, then switched to stand-up comedy and started writing plays 'when the punchlines ran out'. Her first play *Cat and Mouse* was performed in 1987, followed by *Adult Child/Dead Child* (1988, Time Out Award), *Why Is John Lennon Wearing A Skirt?* (1991, London Fringe Award), *Death and Dancing*, *Drag Act*, *Leaking From Every Orifice* and is currently working on her next performance project, *All Over Lovely*. Other work includes *Came Out, It Rained, Went Back In Again* (1992, BBC2, part of City Shorts season); *Kevin* (1994, Central Children's Television); *The Year of the Monkey* (1995, BBC Radio 3). She was awarded an Arts Council bursary in 1995 to write *Easy Access (for the Boys)*, a play without a part in it for her.

Methuen Drama **Modern Plays**

First published in Great Britain in 1996
by Methuen Drama

5 7 9 10 8 6 4

Adult Child / Dead Child was first published in 1988 by Methuen Drama in *Plays by
Women: Seven* copyright © 1988 by Claire Dowie
Why Is John Lennon Wearing a Skirt?, *Death and Dancing*, *Drag Act*, *Leaking From
Every Orifice* copyright © 1996 by Claire Dowie
The author has asserted her moral rights

ISBN 0 413 71090 4

A CIP catalogue record for this book is available from the British Library

Typeset by Wilmaset Ltd, Birkenhead, Wirral

Claire Dowie

Why Is John Lennon Wearing A Skirt
and other stand-up theatre plays

Methuen Drama

Contents

Adult Child/Dead Child

Adult Child/Dead Child was first presented at the Finborough Theatre Club, London, on 5 June 1987, before touring nationally.

Performed by Claire Dowie
Directed by Colin Watkeys

Author's Note
Adult Child/Dead Child was written without gender in mind and can therefore be performed by either sex.

When you are a child
and you don't get any love, when there is no love
when you get this feeling that you can't explain
this feeling that's inside you but you can't explain
you don't know what it is, you can't say it's lack of love
because you don't have those words
you only have the feeling but you don't have those words
those words that say nobody loves me. I am unloved
all you have is the feeling
and the feeling is an empty feeling, a hole in your stomach
you feel this hole in your stomach that you can't explain
because you don't have the words, only the feeling, the
empty feeling
and the feeling hurts, you feel hurt because you can't explain
you feel hurt and frustrated that there is no love
and you can't explain, you feel trapped in your feelings
trapped in your feelings of hurt and frustration and lack of love
lack of love that makes you hit out.

Clean house, tidy house
spotless
nothing out of place
except me
can't seem to please them
can't win for losing
my mother despaired of me
I despaired of me.
My sister was an angel
never put a foot wrong
always clean, always tidy
a perfect child, a joy to behold.

A spotless, squeaky-clean hall floor
muddy shoes tramped from school
footprints – my mother's anger
my mother's annoyance
I would've walked on the ceiling if I could

like spiderman
but I expect the ceiling was squeaky-clean too.

My father was an actor
professional pretender
pretended to be a father
pretended to have feelings
pretended enthusiasm
demanded perfection
demanded perfection
One hundred per cent do it right, do it the best
be brainy, be sporty, be talented, be good
academic athlete
well-mannered, polite, know it all, do it all
One hundred per cent do it right, do it the best
I cried, I would cry
I would cry and I failed
always failed
for my professional pretending father
and his daughter, the apple of his eye
who could do no wrong.

I remember being in the garden of our old house. I was about
six or seven and there were friends of my parents visiting. I
can't remember now who, but somebody gave me a cowboy
and Indian set. This was a cowboy hat and gun and holster
and a tin star with the word 'sheriff' on it and an Indian
feather thing with a band on it for a hat and a tomahawk and
my dad said let's play with it and first he was the cowboy and
I was the Indian and everybody was watching and I ran at
him with my tomahawk but he shot me so I lost and then we
changed round and I was the cowboy and my dad was the
Indian but before I could shoot him he threw the tomahawk
and it hit my head and he said it was Custer's last stand and
everybody laughed (I thought he said 'custard' and I didn't
understand) and he said I was hopeless because I died twice
and I didn't want to play with my cowboy and Indian set any
more but later on that night I decided to be the Indian and
sneak up on him quietly but when I sneaked into their

bedroom and jumped on him with my tomahawk he woke
up. Didn't act like a cowboy, acted like an angry father.

Clumsy, I was clumsy
I was a clumsy child
knocked things, broke things
a clumsy child
always falling over, breaking things
trying to avoid running into things
swerving round things
trying not to be clumsy
trying to walk through the gap in the doorframe
instead of into the doorframe
trying to stop my body moving before it was too late
it was always too late
I was a clumsy child
clumsy.

Never a day would go by that I wasn't walking into things,
tripping up, knocking things over and banging and crashing
my way about the house. It worried me. It drove my parents
crazy.
Fidgeting was another habit I couldn't seem to shake off
which annoyed my parents intensely. Once my dad got so
mad about it that he tied me down rigidly to a chair for a
while. Strangely it didn't stop me feeling fidgety, just stopped
me being fidgety.

And the cupboard, the cupboard under the stairs
I wasn't abused
I was never what you'd call an abused child
not abused
not by any stretch of the imagination
but there was the cupboard, the cupboard under the stairs
dark, silent, claustrophobic
nothing to do, nothing to say, nothing to be but lifeless,
invisible
nowhere, nothing
sitting in the cupboard till I 'learn to behave myself and show
some respect'

in the cupboard under the stairs
and eye for eye and tooth for tooth punishments
my parents were great believers in
'see how you like it'
eye for eye and tooth for tooth punishments
I was never abused
not what you'd call an abused child
not abused
everything I got I deserved
except the cupboard, the cupboard under the stairs
I never locked anyone in a cupboard
but my parents did.

I remember when we moved I was about eight and my sister
and I went to stay with friends of my parents for a week,
probably to get us out of the way while the moving was sorted
out. The friends of my parents had a son called Andrew, who
was I think, a couple of years older and when nobody was
around he'd punch me and pinch me. His parents wouldn't
believe me.
Before we moved I asked my mum where London was and
she said it was a hundred miles away. I was very worried
about it, staying with these friends of my parents and
Andrew. A hundred miles is a long way to run when you're
eight.
I remember being very relieved that there wasn't a cupboard
under the stairs at our new flat in London. Then I found out
there was a broom cupboard which was much smaller.

You want to hit out because of this lack of love that you can't
explain
so you hit out because of this lack of love
you hit out at the people around you
hit out at the people, the adults around you
the adults around you when you are a child
because when you are a child the adults have the power
the adults have the power and they know everything
they know everything so they know your feelings
adults understand feelings, they can explain your feelings
because adults have the power to explain feelings

to know what you are feeling so you hit out
you hit out because they won't help you with your feelings
because you have these feelings but they won't help
they won't help you with these empty feelings
these empty feelings that hurt but you can't explain
this hurt and frustration because you can't explain
so you stop trusting the adults.

My invisible friend
a voice in my head
I could talk to her
I played with her
we understood each other
she was reliable.
She came I think when I was four or five
or maybe earlier, who knows
but by the age of seven
she was with me always
chattering away, making jokes
telling stories
poking fun at family and visitors
making me laugh at all times
at lonely times, good times
boring times, embarrassing times
and awkward times
when I giggled
and my parents wondered about me
and punished me for being bad-mannered
impolite or stupid

I didn't give my invisible friend a name till I was eight. I
don't know why, I don't know why she was a girl either, she
just was and she was just nameless till we moved to London. I
hated London. I hated the school I had to go to because they
beat me up because I talked funny. I hated the flat we'd
moved to because it was smaller and so was the cupboard.
And I hated the street where we lived because it was snobby
and stuck up but I loved my lady. My lady lived down the
road from us and she was always pottering around her front
garden with her dog Benji, stopping to chat to people as they

passed including me. She called me 'scallywag' and she
smiled and spoke nicely to me. She made me feel special and I
loved her even though I didn't know what 'scallywag'
meant, but I knew it was a nice name because she also called
Benji a scallywag and I could tell that she loved him very
much and never hurt or ignored him even though she also
called him a monster and a horror and a terror. I would
spend hours sometimes going up and down the road so that
my lady could say 'hello, scallywag' and I could say 'hello'
back. Sometimes she would say 'off on your travels,
scallywag?' when I passed and sometimes she would say
'jaunting again, scallywag?'. One thing she never asked was
why I was always walking up and down the road.
One day I was coming down the road trying to make up my
mind if I was travelling or jaunting when I passed my next-
door neighbours, the Bannermans. They had been talking to
my lady and as I passed I overheard Mr Bannerman say
'she's a stupid old cow, isn't she'.

Well, I was angry. I was angry
I was so upset and too confused
to look her in the eye and say hello
I was just so angry
I had to run, had to pass her
couldn't stop, couldn't smile
I just ran, just so angry
what he said, how could he say that
about my lady, my lovely lady
just got so upset, so angry
couldn't say hello, couldn't pretend to smile
just had to run
just had to run to my house and sit in My Place
just had to run and sit in My Place.

(My Place incidentally was the narrow gap between the shed
and the fence where nobody thought of looking.)

And I sat in My Place and my invisible friend sat in My Place
and we fumed about the Bannermans and my invisible friend
said 'Something's got to be done'. I agreed but didn't know

what, so we sat in silence for a while till my invisible friend
decided that if they were going down the road (which they
were) it must mean that they were going out, and if they were
going out (which they must have been) then that means that
they're not in and if they are not in (which they weren't) then
we should put a brick through their window and since I can't
because I'm invisible (which she was) then you'll have to do
it (which I didn't want to do because it was wrong and I was
scared). This was when we started arguing and my invisible
friend told me that if I didn't put a brick through the
Bannerman's window she was going to go away and never
speak to me again.

My invisible friend
the voice in my head
I talked to her
I played with her
we understood each other
she was reliable.
She threatened to leave
she said she'd go
I was only eight
I didn't realise what was happening
what was beginning
I was just scared at that point
of loneliness
of immediate loneliness
I didn't realise what was happening
what was beginning
what would happen later on
but that was the starting point
that's when I began to lose control.

So of course finally I had to agree and finally I did put a brick
through the Bannermans' window after making sure first
that my father was still out and my mother was engrossed in
the hoovering. So I threw a brick through the Bannermans'
window. After I'd thrown the brick and heard the glass
shatter I ran back to My Place and waited five or ten minutes
to see if the sky would fall in or (worse) my father would

appear. It didn't and he didn't and nobody started shouting
and nothing happened and everything was still all right even
though I'd done a wrong thing. And not only that but I also
felt triumphant and happy and giggled uncontrollably for
ages. My invisible friend giggled uncontrollably too and
then she told me she had loads of ideas that would be really
funny to do in the future. I wasn't so sure and asked her if
they were wrong things but she just giggled some more and
said 'wait and see'. So it was then that I decided that my
invisible friend was really, when all was said and done, a
monster and a horror and a terror and I called her Benji.

You stop trusting the adults because they have the power
they have the power but won't help
so you don't trust them, they are against you
they are against you because they won't help
and they have the power to help but they won't
so you don't trust them, because they won't help
so you start to hate them because you don't trust them
you start to hate them because they won't help
you hit out because you hate them

My parents had always known about my invisible friend. She
sat next to me at the dinner table (and she didn't like
cabbage either). Occasionally, through me she'd ask them a
question, they'd answer. By the time I was eight and had
called her Benji, they were telling me I was too old for
imaginary friends. Stupid. Benji was still there, I could hear
her, I could feel her, she talked to me, I played with her, and
we did things together.

Little things, easy things
so what if that ornament got broken
it just sat there anyway
didn't do anything
and if they asked me well
I dunno, wasn't me
I was nowhere near it
and what money?
I don't know anything about any money

and so what if my sister lost her charm bracelet
it was a horrible charm bracelet
it rattled
anyway I don't know
maybe she just dropped it somewhere
maybe it just fell off
I don't know.

We got away with it for a long time, mostly because Benji was
a good liar and would tell me what to say if anyone asked.
One day my mother said:

You just broke that picture.
What?
You just broke it.
No I didn't.
Yes you did, I saw you.
No, it was an accident.
No it wasn't, I saw you.
It was an accident.
You picked it up and threw it on the floor.
No I didn't.
I just saw you.
It was an accident.
I saw you.
Benji did it.
Oh, don't be so stupid.
She did.
Will you stop that Benji stuff, it was you.
No, it was Benji.
Look, it was you, now just stop it, you're too old for all that
rubbish.
But she did.

I was too old for imaginary friends but Benji was still with
me, even so I got the blame, and the cupboard for telling lies.

And so it started.

Slowly
a little bit at a time
a little more each day

moving away further and further
making it more difficult to understand each other
making it more difficult to try
they were far away from me over that side: parents, sister,
teachers
everybody.
Benji and I were on this side
My lady I could still reach, still connect with, she was in the
middle.
But then she left.

I knew she was leaving she told me
I was sad about it but didn't show it
Just wanted to buy her a leaving present
a remembrance of me
a dog
an ornament of a dog
but it was expensive, couldn't afford it
had no money
couldn't afford anything with no money.
Benji got hold of some money
we bought the dog the day before
give it to her in the morning
we said, we thought
I got up early especially
I was washed, I was dressed
I didn't want any breakfast.

But then my mother starts.
She's going on and on about some money missing from her
purse, she wants to know, my dad joins in, my sister sits there
all innocent and perfect, they're on at me, on at me, I don't
want to know, not now, I just want to go up the road and give
my lady her present, I can't be bothered with this money
business right now, when I get home from school fair enough,
but not now, its getting on my nerves all their questions,
accusations, fingers pointing in my face, Benji's getting
annoyed, Benji's getting angry, I can feel her, not now, I
don't want this kind of thing now, I just want to go up the
road and give my lady her present, she's leaving, I've got to

give it to her before she leaves, before it's too late. My mother going on and on, my father poking his nose in, my sister sitting there smug and silent, Benji goes mad, I can't control her. I've lost control of her, can't control her outburst, it's not helping, my parents have really got something to say now, really got it in for me now, and I don't want this. I just want to go up the road before she leaves.

I didn't know her name, I never did know her name. I don't think she knew mine either, she just called me 'scallywag' and I was happy with that. I couldn't explain it to my parents, I couldn't tell them about her, never had, she was my secret, they didn't know and if I'd tried to explain they would probably have thought I was making it up as an excuse or something, a lie, and they certainly wouldn't have believed that it was Benji who took the money.

My dad drove me to school that morning because I was late with all the arguing. I didn't bother listening to his lecture, just looked out of the window with my hand in my pocket holding the ornament. I couldn't see too much of my lady's house as we passed it because of the big Pickford's van in front but I caught a glimpse of Benji pissing against the tree in the garden. When I came home from school the house was empty, my lady was gone, I'd missed her. I didn't know what to do with the ornament so I posted it through her letterbox. I heard it break as it hit the floor (no carpets). It didn't matter, I had no use for it anyway.

You build a wall of anger and mistrust and hatred
and you build a wall because they wouldn't help you
and you hate these adults because they made you build a wall
they made you build a wall of hatred because they wouldn't help
and you hit out because they made you build the wall
you hit out in hatred because of the wall that you built
and the wall gets stronger because your hatred grows
and your hatred grows as awareness comes.

Further and further away, no understanding, no communication. Just me and Benji in our own little world and all the rest of them in theirs. Miles apart and no bridges.

The only time our worlds collided was when Benji did
something wrong and I got the blame for it.
At school I had to see a child psychologist. (What an idiot.)

Benji loved words like outlaw, hooligan, gangster,
delinquent, vandal – she thought they sounded good,
romantic, exciting.

Benji would swear. It wouldn't have been so bad if it was just
swearing, if it was just swearing, if Benji just swore, it
wouldn't have been so bad. But it wasn't, wasn't just
swearing, Benji stole. She stole. She stole money, from my
parents, from my school mates, from everybody, she needn't,
she didn't have to, she didn't need it. And shoplifting,
shoplifting and stealing things, silly things, she didn't need
them, she stole a toy car once, she didn't need it, she didn't
even like it, she threw it away later, and travelling, going off
jaunting, playing truant from school, not turning up, just
jaunting off anywhere, travelling around. And she shouted.
And she shouted at people and threw things, she'd go mad
and shout at people and throw things, tantrums, she had
tantrums and shouted at people and threw things, threw
things at the wall, all over the room, threw the furniture and
the ornaments at the walls and all over the room and at
people, she threw things at people and shouted at them and
swore at them, she swore, it wouldn't have been so bad if she
just swore but she didn't. She was wild, uncontrollable. She
thought it was funny. I didn't. I never wanted to get into
trouble, I never did want to get into all that trouble. They
wouldn't believe me that it was Benji so I stopped telling
them. It was just trouble all the time, trouble all the time and
Benji was laughing. I couldn't control her. I couldn't stop
her. She scared me.

Mr Kent
he was a woodwork teacher
and a bastard
by now I was thirteen
and hated by everybody
including Mr Kent

it was about a year since my lady left
and I'd been at war with Benji on and off since then
I was at war with Benji
and everybody was at war with me.
I was making a toast rack in woodwork
Mr Kent said I was an idiot
I was proud of my toast rack
Mr Kent said it was crap
Mr Kent said I was useless
Mr Kent said I was a worthless specimen of a human being
Mr Kent went on and on and on
till Benji jumped out
and threw a hammer at him.

Everybody was further away from me. Everybody and
everything way off in the distance. I couldn't connect at all,
not at all. I didn't even know how to try. I didn't know
anything because I was on this side, way over here and Benji,
Benji was in the middle now, in control. Benji was in control
of everything now, and I hated her.

Luckily it missed
but I was sent to the headmaster
he started shouting
but I couldn't understand
couldn't make sense of it.
Benji understood cus she was answering him
but I don't know what she said
because I couldn't understand
couldn't make sense of it
I doubt if she was apologising though.
I'm aware that he's phoning my parents
I don't understand what's happening
I'm aware that they're out
because he doesn't talk to the telephone.

He says they will be contacted
and asked to come to the school
it's filtering through but it makes no sense.
Benji understands cus she's smirking

I am aware of that.
I get sent home
I go home
in the evening they get the phone call
they are asked to go but they don't know why
just that they have to discuss me
I am to be discussed
they have to go to discuss me
they asked me why
I didn't answer
I said I don't know
because I didn't, really
it doesn't make sense
but I am aware
that they are looking at me
with hatred.

All night, it was a long night, it was black and then it was dawn. All night, a long night, I am awake, or sort of awake, or something, I'm not sure, I don't know what's happening with me. Benji doesn't stop talking, doesn't stop telling me that my dad's going to kill me when he finds out, all night, I can't sleep. Benji won't shut up, I don't know what's happening to me, I can't seem to sort anything out, I can't seem to understand anything, all night, and Benji keeps telling me, keeps talking, an eye for an eye, he's going to kill you when he finds out, all night, a long night, such a long night, and Benji telling me over and over, remember when you kicked your sister how he kicked you, remember when you threw stones at those boys how he threw stones at you, an eye for an eye, tooth for tooth, remember when you broke his record, he broke your toys, remember when you broke his wing mirror he broke your bike, eye for eye, tooth for tooth, remember when you smashed the radio he smashed your record player, remember when you wrecked the living room he wrecked your bedroom, all night, all night, and I never did those things, I never did, Benji did them, it was Benji, I don't know what's happening. I don't, and the cupboard after, the cupboard after, the cupboard, cupboard, he's going to kill you, see how you like it, remember the ashtray, the ashtray, you threw it at him, it was the same, you threw the ashtray, remember it didn't hit him did it, it didn't hit him, but he was going to hit you wasn't he, he was, you could tell couldn't you, ah yes, you could tell, he was going to hit you with the ashtray, wasn't he, he was, she stopped him, remember she stopped him, she said don't, and she stopped him, but he was going to, he was going to hit you with the ashtray remember he was, he would have if she hadn't stopped him, and now look what you've done. I didn't do anything, it was you, you threw it, it was you, you did it, but they won't believe you will they, they never do, they never did, you threw the hammer, what's he going to do, think about it, what's he going to do. I can't think, shut up please, leave me alone, eye for eye, tooth for tooth, you threw the hammer, what's he going to do, think about it, he's going to kill you when he finds out, he's going to kill you, eye for eye, and tooth for tooth, remember and then the cupboard, what're you going to do, what are you going to do now, remember, remember the ashtray, he's going to kill you now that's what, unless you kill him first, unless you do it first, to save yourself, to defend yourself, eye for eye, defend yourself, tooth for tooth, when he finds out, what are you going to do, you're going to die that's what you'll do, when he finds out, you'll die, he'll kill you, he'll kill you when he finds out, eye for eye, tooth for tooth, you've got to defend yourself, you've got to find the hammer first, before he finds out, you've got to find the hammer, you've got to defend yourself, eye for eye, tooth for tooth, and then the cupboard, and then the cupboard, find the hammer, eye for eye he's going to kill you when he finds out, remember, remember the ashtray, remember, all night, all night, it was a long night, all night and I don't know. I can't understand any more. I don't know what's happening to me and Benji won't shut up. And I do remember the ashtray. I do remember that. I do remember that she stopped him. And I don't know anymore. I can't understand, I can't think right. I don't know and it's all night, all night, it's black and then it's dawn and then I'm there in their bedroom with the hammer and I don't know

how. I don't know. I don't understand and then I hit him
with it. I hit him. I don't understand. I don't know what's
happening. And then he wakes up, he wakes up.

He woke up.
I hit him.
I caught him on the head and he woke up
it woke him, it hurt.
I dropped the hammer
I turned and left the room
left the flat
I went travelling
Benji took me travelling
we went miles
I don't know where we went
we just travelled
and the police picked me up
my mom fetched me
after the police had phoned
it was late, they found me wandering
I was just travelling, just jaunting
Benji took me, we just went
and then my mom picked me up
collected me from the police station
and brought me home
and she stopped at a shop and bought me a Mars bar and a
packet of crisps
and I knew then that I'd be in the cupboard all night
and it didn't matter.

You start to hit out in hatred because they have the power
you hit out in hatred but you still can't explain
you still can't explain because they've never helped you
they had the power but they never helped you
so you hit out in hatred but you can't explain
you can't explain this hatred, this feeling of hatred
this feeling of hatred and mistrust for these people
these adults who had the power but wouldn't help
so you build a wall around you.

Lunatic
lunacy
loony
mad
insane
I didn't know anything about psychiatrists
or mental health
or anything
except what I'd heard
and read
and watched on television.

Deranged
psychopath
psycho.

And then I had to see one
had to see a psychiatrist
not for hitting my dad
but for hitting
myself
loony
mad
crazy.

It was mad. Totally out of hand. I didn't know what else to
do really. I was under virtual house arrest at home, it was
barmy. I'd been suspended from school for two weeks
because Mr Kent and the headmaster couldn't take a joke,
well all right, it wasn't funny, no, it was very dangerous, but
it had missed and he had asked for it. Anyway my parents
decided to keep an eye on me. I think basically they were
scared stiff of me. I don't blame them really I was pretty
loopy around that time, but if anything's guaranteed to drive
you mad it's having your parents and sister tiptoeing around
the place, glancing sidelong at you all the time, locking your
bedroom door every night, not saying anything about
anything, and then trying to pretend that nothing's
happened and everything's hunky dory. We should have
talked about it, somebody should have said something, done

something, anything. I was feeling terrible about it, I didn't know what to do, how to apologise. Nothing happened, nobody said a word, nobody did a thing, they just watched me, kept me in the house, hardly spoke a word to me and watched me, and locked my bedroom door at night. What could I do, how could I explain, it was mad, it was driving me mad, and Benji. I had to put up with Benji. I could feel her bubbling under all the time with all the tension. I knew she was going to explode soon if something didn't happen. She couldn't bear it. I couldn't bear it, we couldn't go on like that, with my parents tiptoeing around not knowing what to do with me, being scared of me, watching me, my dad sitting there with a big purple bruise on his head as if nothing had happened. And Benji inside me, bubbling, beginning to get restless, starting to rage about the atmosphere. Couldn't go on like that, somebody had to do something, somebody had to make a move, stop the tension, do something before Benji did. So I did. I did something. I did what they wanted to do, did what my dad should have done, get it over with, get it out of the way, clear the air, make amends, even the score, so, eye for eye, tooth for tooth. I hit myself with the hammer. That made something happen, made somebody say something, do something. It did. They sent me to a psychiatrist.

Lunatic.

I was scared. I was scared because the psychiatrist was asking me questions, talking to me and making complete sense to me. I could understand what he was getting at. I thought I'm not going to answer otherwise he'll find out I'm a loony and he'll put me in the snake pit.

The Snake Pit.
I saw a film once called *The Snake Pit*
it was a film about a loony bin
it was horrible, awful, scary
I was scared to go to the Snake Pit
I thought I'd get sent to the Snake Pit
get put in the Snake Pit
in the loony bin

couldn't answer his questions or he'd know
he'd know I was loony
and I'd get put in the loony bin
in the Snake Pit.

And he asked about the hammer, and I got scared then. He
said first you tried to hammer the woodwork teacher, then
you hammered your father, then you hammered yourself.

Norman Bates
Jekyll and Hyde
the Boston Strangler
Crippen and me.

First you tried to hammer the woodwork teacher, then you
hammered your father, then you hammered yourself. Me a
hammer murderer. I wanted to explain that it wasn't how it
sounded, I wanted to explain that it wasn't one, two, three,
hammer, hammer, hammer without a pause for breath, like
he was saying it, like I was a hammer murderer on the
rampage. I wanted to explain that it didn't happen like that
and then he said, 'Why did you choose a hammer?'.

Oh lord, I was scared then
I had to say over and over
I didn't choose a hammer
I never chose a hammer
it wasn't that I chose a hammer.

Norman Bates
Jekyll and Hyde
the Boston Strangler
Crippen and me
the hammer murderer
all in the Snake Pit
together.

(I was getting scared.)

I went to the psychiatrist and we all went to family therapy,
and my parents talked and my sister talked and I said
nothing, and when the therapist asked me anything I said I

dunno. And I sat in the sessions like I sat in the cupboard just
waiting for the time to go round.

And the weeks passed and the time went round.

And my parents slowly stopped pressing me
and my parents slowly stopped getting at me
and my parents slowly stopped nagging and criticising me
and my parents slowly stopped punishing me
my parents slowly stopped.
And the school was tipped off and eased off
and my sister called me a loony when no one was around
and when the therapist asked if things were better
I said yes.
And they never asked about Benji
and then I stopped going to the psychiatrist.

And the weeks passed and the time went round.

And when Benji and I felt like travelling we went.
And I didn't get into trouble any more
and I never went into the cupboard again
and the eye for eye retributions stopped
and my schoolwork wasn't that important any more
in fact my schoolwork wasn't important at all
nobody asked
and my parents expected nothing from me
and my sister called me a loony when no one was around
and the teachers chose to ignore me
and I chose to ignore the teachers
and Benji still sometimes stole but not often
and Benji still sometimes swore but only quietly
and we travelled a lot
and the time went round
and it still wasn't right.

You become aware of your lack of love
the lack of love you had as a child
you are aware of the lack of love as a child
and the anger grows because you are aware of the lack of love
and the wall gets stronger as awareness grows
the anger grows and the wall gets stronger

because you are aware of the lack of love
and the wall gets stronger and the anger grows
because you are aware of the adult power
you are aware of adult power and the lack of love
and the anger grows and the wall gets stronger
because frustration comes.

When I was seventeen I thought the best thing to do was get
out, get away, leave home.
I had always been a disappointment to my parents, a waste
of effort, now I was a waste of space.
They let me do what I liked, put up with me, made me feel
guilty.
It would be better. I would feel better. I could sort myself
out. I could be happy.
I thought.

It wasn't like that.

I lived in a bedsit
at first I had a job and then I didn't
I had no job, no money, no friends
I sat in my bedsit
my parents were quite good
sent me the odd tenner
through the post
never visited
I sat in my bedsit
sat in my bedsit
and slowly
went mad in my bedsit.

It started off fine, I felt good, relieved, relaxed. I had no
television but I wasn't worried, I had the library and I had
Benji. She could come and go as she pleased now. I no longer
had to be careful of her coming or going. I was no longer
guarded, or worried of how she or I would appear to others,
there were no others. I sat and talked for hours with Benji,
talking about the past and the future, how much better
things were, a million things we talked about and we laughed
a lot and went travelling, travelling was cheap, we ate what

we wanted to eat when we wanted to eat it and if we didn't
feel like getting up in the morning we didn't.
Occasionally I would think that I was too old for imaginary
friends, but mostly I didn't think about it at all. It started off
fine. I felt good, relieved, relaxed. Then Benji started getting
restless, I could feel her, things weren't really good, things
weren't really all right, we weren't happy. We started
arguing and she got on my nerves as I got on her nerves and
we argued and we weren't happy, this wasn't what we
wanted. And we'd sit in silence for hours, sit in silence, sit in a
chair in silence, sit in a chair in a bedsit in silence for hours.
We went out less and less until we couldn't go out at all,
didn't feel like eating, didn't feel like reading, didn't feel like
travelling, didn't feel like talking. Sat in a chair in a bedsit in
silence for hours. Benji was restless, she said the bedsit was
just a big cupboard, we were just sitting in a big cupboard
waiting for the time to go round and it was claustrophobic,
we ought to get out, go travelling, do something. We sat in a
chair in a bedsit in silence for hours and couldn't move
couldn't get out, couldn't raise the energy. Benji was restless,
started shouting, arguing, the neighbours complained and
Benji got more restless, started arguing with them, started
singing at the top of her voice in the middle of the night. The
neighbours complained more and banged the walls and the
door. Benji swore and shouted and banged back. And the
neighbours complained and banged and threatened and
argued and Benji shouted and sang and swore and screamed
at all hours of the day and night and then the police came and
I was sectioned.
Mental hospitals aren't that bad, they're not bad at all,
quite nice really, and not a bit like the Snake Pit. I was
there for six weeks and they gave me some drugs to calm me
down and I did calm down and I relaxed and Benji calmed
down and faded a bit and I got a grip of myself and felt a
lot better. Everybody (well, nearly everybody) was very
nice and friendly and all the staff, the doctors and nurses
and therapists and everybody said that if I had a problem I
could always talk to them about it, which was very nice of
them, very kind. There were a lot of people in that place

that I could talk to if I had a problem. But I kept quiet and got calmer and got a grip of Benji and myself and felt better.

My parents and sister visited me once.
That was embarrassing.

And then out
with a promise
to keep taking the medication
and go to outpatients
and do a little gardening job
and stay in the hostel.
It was decided
I should live in a hostel
be independent
but have help
close by
if required
somebody there
if I needed them
if I had a problem
if I had another breakdown.

The hostel warden was a bloke called Peter. Peter never once said if I had a problem I could talk to him about it. Peter never once assumed that I had a problem. Peter never mentioned problems either to me or to the other ex-patients. Peter would just chat. Anytime, all the time, whenever. Peter helped.
Peter was a friend, all the people in the hostel were friends, it was a very friendly atmosphere. I liked it. I felt like seven ex-mental patients, a few staff members and Peter were my family. An odd family. A friendly family though.

And I lived with them for two years
and Benji was there
in the background at first
cus of the drugs
but as I slowly felt better
more secure

less in need
false security
I stopped taking them
thought I could manage without them
so Benji got stronger
more prominent
more out front
but friendly though
she was friendly for weeks
very popular
no trouble
false security.
Something went wrong
somebody did or said something wrong
or something happened. I'm not sure
but she started
angry, tantrum
flying off, sounding off
the usual
yelling and screaming and swearing
at my friends
my hostel family
at Peter
mostly at Peter
my friend
who stood there blinking
while Benji sounded off
while Benji threw a spanner in the works
while Benji ruined it all again
While Benji upset the balance
upset the family
upset my friends
upset me
cus I thought I'd be thrown out
cus I though I'd be back in the bin
cus I thought she'd never die down
calm down, stay down.

After she'd done her worst, burnt herself out, let me through, let me get control, let me speak, I apologised, tried to, spluttered and stuttered and tried to say sorry. Felt ashamed, felt terrible.

Peter said: we all get angry sometimes, it's natural.
No.
Yes.
No you don't understand.
It's all right, no damage done.
But you don't understand.
Don't worry about it.
But I do.
You shouldn't, it's OK, you were just letting off steam, that's all.
No it isn't . . . it's Benji.

And I told him.

I told him about Benji, I told him all about Benji, how she was, who she was, where she came from, everything. I told him about how I decided to stop taking my medication weeks ago even though I knew I wasn't supposed to. I told him about my family, my real family, my parents always demanding perfection, always expecting everything, how I couldn't do it, how Benji ruined it for me. How I loved my parents, how my parents hated me. I told him about my lady and how I'd loved her and how I missed her even now and I never knew her name. And I told him about everything, everything I could think of just came pouring out for hours and hours all day. He listened. He listened and never once said I was too old for imaginary friends and he never said I was a loony and he never said I shouldn't have stopped taking the drugs, he listened, and over the days afterwards when I wanted to say some more he listened. And when sometimes it was garbled and didn't make sense he still listened but just asked me to speak slower because he wanted to know because he wanted to listen. And I told him. He never once said I was too old for imaginary friends, he never once said I was loony, he never once said I shouldn't have

stopped taking the drugs, he said once that maybe Benji was
only expressing what I felt. I didn't understand at first but it
made me think about it.

It made me think a lot.

Frustration comes because you are no longer a child
you are no longer a child but you feel like a child
you feel like a child because you need love like a child
you need love like a child because the child needed love
and the anger grows because the child needed love
and the anger grows because you need love like a child
and the anger grows because you are an adult
and the anger grows because frustration comes
and frustration comes because you are an adult
you are an adult but the child needs love
and the anger grows and the wall won't break
and the wall won't break because the anger won't stop
and the anger won't stop because you need love like a child
the child needs love to stop the anger
and you need love like a child to break the wall
you need to break the wall and stop the anger but you can't
say
you can't say you need love like a child
you can't say because you are an adult
you can't say, you can't ask for love like a child
you can't ask because you are adult.

I know now that I'm too old for imaginary friends, I know
that now.
I went back on the medication after the little upset at the
hostel, felt it was for the best.
And then I got a flat, after the hostel, felt I was ready, too old
for imaginary friends, hadn't needed Benji, hadn't even
thought about Benji, I had real friends now, proper ones, not
imaginary, and my doctor agreed, said I was ready and they
got me a flat, a lovely flat and all my friends from the hostel
and Peter came and helped me decorate and arrange the
furniture, it was good, I felt good, much too old for
imaginary friends.

But I was lonely in my flat
I missed my friends and Peter at the hostel
the noise and the commotion and the friendliness.
I'd visit them though
and they'd visit me, often
but after they'd gone
I couldn't bear it
the emptiness and silence
of just me
I'd never been on my own before
always had Benji
never been on my own.

Then I thought, this is silly, I'm just being silly. I'm sure
everybody feels like this when they move into a new place,
bound to. I've just got to get used to it, bound to feel strange,
just got to keep busy, keep myself occupied, not think about it.

Didn't know what to do
then I thought 'why not go travelling?'
I've always enjoyed travelling
always made me feel better
cheered me up.
But I couldn't
I tried
I did try
but I couldn't go
not without Benji
I missed her
couldn't go without her
Benji *was* travelling
couldn't bear it
I don't know, must have panicked
ran back
something
couldn't travel alone.

I didn't know what to do, couldn't stay in and couldn't go
out. I was beginning to get quite depressed. I was too old for
imaginary friends but I couldn't cope on my own. I felt I just

couldn't do it. And it was just at that point, just at that point when I thought I can't do it, can't cope, have to go back to hospital or something, it was just at that point that I had this brilliant idea.

I thought 'why not get a dog?'
and I did.
I got a dog
and it's been brilliant
best thing I've ever done.
I simply got a dog
and I can go travelling now
we go travelling, we go miles
me and my dog
and it's easy, no problem
I don't worry or panic
I don't even think about it
just off we go
and not dirty streets or buses any more
like with Benji
but parks and commons and places
I feel so healthy now too
I simply got a dog
should have done it years ago.

I'm so happy now, she makes me so happy.

And the flat. It doesn't seem empty or silent or anything now, she doesn't say anything but the flat feels so. I just love it, I love going home to my flat now. And it's all because of my dog.
And she's a real dog, she's not imaginary. She is because I got her from Battersea Dogs' Home and I couldn't imagine that place it's so sad, so it's like I rescued her, felt a real hero straight away.
I'm happy now, she's a great dog.
And it's funny cus ever since I've had her I get this feeling that I'm close to my lady again, not physically or anything I don't mean that cus I don't know where she is or anything, couldn't look her up even don't know her name, but I mean in spirit or something, like we connect again, that she's near me, with me.

I don't know, maybe it's because we've both got dogs, maybe we connect through our dogs or something. I don't know but it's just good to know she's there, with me.

So I'm happy now.

And she's a great dog, not perfect though thank God, nothing pedigree, just a scruffy mongrel type, always into things, a real scallywag. And we do everything together, always together, just like Benji was.

I do sometimes have this urge though, to stop taking the medication, just for a while. I don't mean for ever but just for a little while, just so Benji could meet her. I'd really like Benji to meet her, just to see what she thought, to see if they'd get on, cus I'm sure they would, cus Benji's always liked dogs too, ever since we met my lady and her dog, Benji. In fact Benji was dead proud to be called after Benji the dog, so I'm sure she'd like her. Cus she's a great dog.

I'd also like Benji to come back just one more time, just for the last time, because I feel I want to apologise to her. I feel I need to say sorry, cus I know now that it wasn't Benji really. I know now that it was me really, my anger, my emotion that caused all that trouble, all that wasted time, and I just feel I want to say sorry for blaming her. Cus it wasn't her it was me and I feel awful for blaming her. I mean she was my best friend, she was, she was my best friend and I blamed her all those years, so I would just like to say sorry.

And I'd like to say goodbye.

But I can't. I can't even think about it. I mustn't think about it, cus I'm too old for imaginary friends. I've got to keep taking the medication cus it is for the best, so I shouldn't think about Benji or the past or anything. I should just think about my dog, well I do think about my dog in fact, I do, I concentrate on my dog and try to make her happy, cus she makes me happy, she does, she's a great dog, a real scallywag, always into everything, messing up the flat with her dog hairs and everything, I can't keep the place clean I can't, every time I try to clean the floor or anything she's there with her paw prints all over it. She's a real monster and a horror and a terror she is.

I call her Lady.

It's just a name.

Why Is John Lennon Wearing A Skirt?

Why Is John Lennon Wearing A Skirt? was first presented at the Traverse Theatre, Edinburgh, on 14 August 1990.

Performed by Claire Dowie
Directed by Colin Watkeys

Part One

An old-fashioned desk with bench on the stage.

Music: 'Working Class Hero' by John Lennon

Enter wearing school uniform: skirt, socks, sensible flat shoes, shirt, tie, school blazer, satchel over shoulder. Put satchel on back of seat at desk. Walk forward, address the audience.

(*Shows off uniform.*) This was me at fourteen. I liked being fourteen, fourteen was a great age to be, I could be really grown up or really childish depending on what mood I was in . . . and I was very moody – well, according to my mum. 'You're so moody, you are.' 'Well, what do you expect, mum, I'm only fourteen, it's my hormones – whatever they are.' Mostly I suppose I was childish but I didn't care, I had three best friends, all tomboys, and we went round in a gang. The Fab Four we were known as; 'Here they come, the Fab Four,' 'Watch out, it's the Fab Four.' That was us. Course we started it, we called ourselves the Fab Four first because nobody else would; 'Call us the Fab Four.' 'No, I don't want to,' 'Ah, go on,' 'I don't want to,' 'Call us the Fab Four!' 'All right, you're the Fab Four, now bog off will ya!'

Secretly I named my friends Paul, George and Ringo, but I never told them (I'm not stupid), they just seemed to act like Paul, George and Ringo and that was good enough for me. I was John, of course, although you wouldn't think so to look at me dressed like this – but what could you do, it was compulsory, a school rule. Had its compensations though, like this tie for instance. Loved this tie, it was the first thing I put on in the morning, got up, put my tie on – mind you, it took me half an hour to get my shirt on but . . . when else could you wear a tie without having to answer awkward questions? I wore mine like that though (*Adjusts tie to untidy angle.*) sort of roguish – clever but dishevelled – a very Johnish look I thought. So I was quite happy with the top half of me, quite liked the top half of me. (*Takes off blazer, discards it on floor.*) Unfortunately the bottom half I hated. (*Holds edges of skirt in disgust.*) Five days a week for six years I had to wear this thing and five days a week for six years I wanted to know why, what for, what was the point? A piece of material hanging round your waist. I mean, what could you do in it? Could you play football? (*Kicks imaginary ball and catches skirt between legs.*) Yes, but you had to watch your knickers. Could you dive off your desk onto somebody's back and roll around the floor tussling? (*Jumps off desk and rolls around floor clutching skirt between legs.*) Yes, but you had to watch your knickers. Could you slump in your chair, bored and rebellious like James Dean? (*Slumps at desk, legs askew before adjusting skirt.*) Yes, but you had to watch your knickers. You always had to watch your knickers. And of course you got the boys watching your knickers for you – (*Pulls up skirt.*) 'Whooo!' The Knicker Factor I called it. Why was it compulsory, a school rule to implement the Knicker Factor? Why couldn't we wear long ones down to the ankles, all sewn up, covered up and protected like the boys? Took all four of us and a lot of fighting to catch a glimpse of a boy's knickers – two on the arms, one sitting on the feet and one to pull down the trousers – and it was a lot more fun. I wouldn't have minded if we'd worn short ones (*Holds skirt between legs.*) sort of semi-protected, in fact I did that once in needlework, instead of making an oven mitt, sewed it straight up the middle. Felt good, felt really clever, but I got told to stop it, got told to unpick it, got told, 'You'll ruin your skirt.' 'I know, that's the point!' Hated it. (*Skirt.*) Could never figure it out. The only conclusion I came up with was that they made it a school rule just to get at me, just to irritate me. And of course I thought I was right because I was fourteen, and at fourteen I knew everything – well, according to my mum I did. (*Sarcastic.*) 'Oh, you think you know everything, don't you?' 'Yes, Mum, I do.' Unfortunately though, as the term progressed I realised I knew nothing.

Takes off shoes and socks, discards them on floor.

My best friends, Paul, George and Ringo, the Fab Four, we went round in a gang, tomboys, until these walked into the classroom (*Takes out pair of tights from satchel and holds them*

aloft.) on Paul's legs! (*Puts tights on as talking.*) I thought they
looked silly, I thought they looked cold. I said to her, 'What
are you doing for heaven's sake that's the sort of thing my
mum wears, and she's practically forty-six.' And as if that
wasn't bad enough then Ringo started wearing them – just
because Paul did, and then even George . . . the Quiet One!
(*Tights on by now.*) And then when this happened to Paul
(*Pulls up skirt.*) 'Whooo!' I was up, I was ready, ready to jump
on the boy and Knicker Factor him. But what did Paul do?
She went: (*Folds arms and looks 'adultly' irritated.*) 'Oh, for
heaven's sake why don't you just grow up, you stupid boy!'
(*Pause, stunned.*) Well, where's the fun in that? There is none.
Something started happening to my friends – 'Do you want a
game of football?' 'Nah.' 'Want a game of wrestling?' 'Nah.'
'Well, do you wanna just slouch around then?' 'Nah, I think
I'll just sit like this thanks.' (*Sits at desk in a ladylike fashion,
smiling, with toes placed on ground.*) Toe ache. They must have
got toe ache, because they started wearing these (*Takes out
heeled court shoes from satchel and puts them on, walks around ladylike
before standing still and rolling up skirt.*) Then they must have
started thinking their legs looked really good, they must have
thought their legs looked marvellous, because they started
doing this. (*Finishes rolling with skirt really short, almost showing
knickers.*) Now what can you do? (*Tries raising leg, bending over,
stretching etc., without showing knickers.*) Nothing. Well, you
could stand there, looking pretty and showing everybody
your legs, I suppose. (*Stands for a while.*) Gets a bit boring
after a while though. So what's the point of that? And then I
noticed something. The Knicker Factor. They've taken the
Knicker Factor to extremes. They've made it so that they're
almost showing their knickers all the time, but we never
actually see their knickers again. Ever. Because for some
reason the boys go nowhere near them, the boys avoid them
like the plague, the boys are suddenly scared stiff of them.
Wow! And my friends stand there saying, 'Go on, I dare you,
go on.' And they don't! Brilliant. But it's a bit drastic, isn't it?
A bit restrictive. (*Starts unrolling skirt.*) Still, that's all right,
I've got my skirt down to my knees and my socks up to my

knees, but we're still best friends, still a gang, we're still getting on all right.

However, I'm not getting on all right with my mother. (*Takes off skirt and discards it on floor. Starts putting on jeans from desk.*) My mother is suggesting that I be a bit more glamorous. That it would be a good idea if we both went into town so that she could help me choose some clothes. 'I don't think so, Mum, I mean, after all you are practically forty-six, aren't you.' She thinks it's not such a good idea for me to play football any more since I might get kicked in the stomach and drop my womb. (*Puts on socks from desk and flat school shoes from floor.*) She thinks my hair could do with a bit of body – which bit? An arm, a leg? – my face could do with a bit of colour and she thinks pink would suit me – 'But I don't like pink, Mum.' 'But it suits you.' 'But I don't like it.' 'Well, you're going to have to learn to like it because it suits you.' She says I'd do better if I pulled my shoulders back, sat properly and didn't slouch – do better at what? Sitting? I've done that since I was two and I haven't fallen over yet. And every time I go anywhere she says, 'Watch the buses, don't talk to any strange men, don't let the boys get away with it, remember you're a nice girl from a nice home and have you got a clean handkerchief?' I'm only going to the pictures with me mates, Mum.

At the pictures there were eight of us; Ringo was snogging very loudly with a boy while Paul and George were tutting and complaining about four lads who were throwing bits of paper around the audience and being obnoxious. The rest of us were throwing bits of paper around the audience and being obnoxious. It didn't occur to me though till I was half way home that girls just don't seem to have fun any more, I mean, they giggle a lot, but they don't do anything.

So I hung around with the boys for a while, waiting for my womb to drop. We played football, said 'fuck' every other word and smoked cigarettes pretending to be adults. Typical lads and I was one of them, or so I thought till we walked past a park bench with three frozen girls on it. They giggled and we stopped. The boys nudged each other, looked shy and kicked the ground while the girls started preening themselves and trying to look aloof. I thought this was barmy, what are they doing? So I sat down next to them and started talking. (*Sits at desk.*) 'Aren't you a bit cold in that strapless thing?' 'Yes I am a bit, I'm frozen actually.' 'Well, why don't you put a cardigan on?' 'Ooh, I couldn't, it would spoil the effect.' (*Giggles.*) 'Been playing football?' 'Yeah.' 'Yeah, I know, we were watching you.' (*Giggles.*) The others are still kicking the ground and being embarrassed, but not me, I think this is great, I think this is perfect because I feel just like John Lennon chatting to a Beatle fan who won't stop giggling, I'm in heaven – until one of the boys pipes up and shouts at the gigglers, 'Oi, she's a girl, you know.' Thank you, they do now. Well, needless to say it was embarrassing, and I was ostracised by the boys from then on. Not my fault I'm better looking than they are.

So it's back to the girls' camp and things are moving apace. (*Tips up satchel with make up in it into the desk.*) 'We're going to a dance on Saturday, do you wanna come?' 'Yeah, all right, what time?' 'Come to my house about two.' 'What time's the dance?' 'Eight.' 'What are we going to do all afternoon?' Stupid me. I turn up like this more or less with a couple of LPs under my arm thinking we're in for a fun afternoon and I end up sitting on the bed singing 'Help' while the other three prepare.

Sings a few lines from 'Help' by the Beatles while propping up the desk lid, which has a mirror inside the lid to turn the desk into a vanity table – sits at table and pretends putting on make up as though the other three.

'Ooh, that's a lovely colour, can I borrow some?' 'Don't nudge me, oh look, I've smudged it now, I'm going to have to start all over again, and it's three o'clock already, I'll never be ready in time.' (*Pulls out toilet roll from desk and starts unravelling strips of it as if to remove make up.*) Even George the Quiet One; (*Mimes lipstick, then blotting it with a piece of toilet paper.*) Finally I say, 'Why are you doing this?' 'You've got to!' 'Wanna borrow some?' 'No thanks.' 'Wanna borrow a

dress?' 'No thanks.' 'Wanna borrow a skirt?' 'No thanks.'
'Touch of lipstick?' 'No.' 'Bit of colour for your cheeks?' 'You
sound like my mother.' 'All right, but you'll be sorry.' 'I
won't.' I was.

At the dance we were laughing and dancing and giggling and
talking, guzzling Coca Cola, smoking cigarettes pretending
to be adults and then the boys arrived. Phoom, all the girls
disappear into the toilets. I didn't know, hadn't been told the
rules. So I sat there and watched the boys prepare; (*Slouches
around trying to find a 'cool' position to pose in, finally settles on the
thumbs through the belt loops look.*) guzzling Coca Cola – 'ta' and
smoking cigarettes pretending to be adults – 'ta'. (*Tries to
smoke and drink with thumbs still in belt loops.*) Then the toilet
door flys open and out all the girls parade. (*Walks around as
though in beauty contest.*) A hundred and one different varieties
of cheap perfume getting to their seats before them. Positions
are taken, girls on one side of the room, boys on the other,
and then it starts. The dance hall turns into a shooting
gallery at a fairground, the boys have the rifles and the girls
are the targets, the sitting ducks. (*Waddles backwards and
forwards, bobbing up and down slightly and smiling like a duck hoping
to get picked.*) Some of the boys take aim and shoot off. (*Runs
from boys' side to girls'.*) 'Would you like to dance?' (*As though
bored rigid.*) 'Oh, all right.' (*Stand in centre and dance, bored, turn
to girls' side momentarily to speak with joy.*) 'I've been picked.'
(*Keeps dancing bored, then to 'girl' pleased.*) 'Isn't he lovely, isn't
he gorgeous?' (*To 'boy'*) 'You're all right I suppose . . . fancy
a snog?' (*Locks arms around 'boy'.*) Some of the boys miss badly.
(*Runs from boys' side.*) 'Would you like to dance?' 'Shove off,
spotty!' Then he can't get back. (*Stiffly tries to get back to boys'
side.*) 'I can't get back.' Sweat pours off him, 'Sweat's
pouring off me.' His eyes bulge, 'Me eyes are bulging.'
Nobody's taking the blindest bit of notice of him,
'Everybody's looking at me and it's three miles!' Finally a
friend rescues him, 'Ugly cow, I only asked her cus I felt sorry
for her!' And so it goes, on and on, all night, till there's only
one left. Me. I shouldn't have to do this, I don't want to do
this, I'm getting a reputation for being ugly. I can't hang

around with the boys any more in case somebody thinks I'm an ugly girlfriend and I can't hang around with the girls any more in case somebody thinks I'm a boyfriend. I tried sitting at home but all I get is sympathetic looks from my parents and a pep talk from my mum, 'No, you're not ugly, you've got a lovely face, you have, it's just like mine. But you've got to do something with it. I mean look at your hair *(Starts messing with hair.)* fluff it up a bit.' 'I don't want it fluffed up, Mum.' *(Messes with cheekbones.)* 'Put a bit of colour on your cheeks, you could look like Audrey Hepburn.' 'I don't want to look like Audrey Hepburn!' 'Well, you've got to glamourize yourself, I did at your age and I could have had any man I chose.' 'Well, why did you choose Dad then?'

(Starts to take clothes off except bra, vest, knickers and tights.) So after the forty-second round of playing sitting ducks at a shooting gallery and never once getting shot, I decided I wasn't happy, I wasn't winning, I'm a little bit lonely and I might be wrong.

Puts on pretty dress and high heels in silence, looking defeated, then sits at desk/vanity table and starts to put on make up.

(While putting on make up.) My first boyfriend stood me up outside the cinema. I say boyfriend although he wasn't technically, since we never actually got together, but when it's your first you've got to say something. My second boyfriend met me outside the cinema, took me in, sat me down and then started grappling with my tits and my mouth – I'm not sure if it was for his benefit or mine, but I wasn't very keen. Missed half the film as well, mostly going: *(Beats off imaginary attacker.)* 'Don't milk me!' My third boyfriend was great on his own, but ninety per cent of the time insisted on us going everywhere with his mates, so that he could talk to them and park me in the corner with half a lager and lime like a trophy. My fourth boyfriend talked to me all the time. I never once got a word in edgeways, he said he loved girls because they were such good listeners. He then said, 'How about it?' My fifth boyfriend was really nice so I said, 'How about it?' but he couldn't get the condom on and said I was

stupid for not being on the Pill and don't I know that all girls
are prepared nowadays? I wondered if he meant prepared
like an oven-ready chicken but I didn't say. My sixth
boyfriend did get the condom on but sex was over in about
thirty seconds and I wondered what the point was since I'd
hardly felt anything except embarrassment about looking
vaguely like a centrefold in a girlie magazine. (*Spreads arms
and legs from sitting position in demonstration.*) My seventh
boyfriend spent a useful couple of hours telling me the
trouble with women was their hormones, their frigidity and
their desperate ambition to get married. We weren't suited,
only lasted a couple of hours. My eighth boyfriend was a
proper gentleman, full of respect for females, did everything
for me – including thinking, which I thought was very nice of
him, since I'd never have been able to do it on my own. My
ninth boyfriend called me a feminist lesbian every time I
disagreed with his opinions and a brainless chick every time I
didn't offer one. My tenth boyfriend was a real
revolutionary, however, even looked like Che Guevara,
believed totally in womens' liberation. But only after the
working-class revolution. I said I presume that's the
working-class male revolution, he said 'Don't nit-pick.' I
said 'I won't, I can't be bothered.'

Finishes making up.

In between times I went dancing with the girls.

*Music: 'Ride A White Swan' by T. Rex. Simple dancing that girls do
all in a line, looking pretty vacant.*

Music fade-out during dialogue.

Or I went to the pictures and saw chicks in the flicks in the
background like a Christmas tree listening to the male talk,
never joining in. Or tarts in small parts, trying to steal the
scene looking sexy with a cigarette. Or dolly birds in
miniskirts working as a secretary, filing their nails and
looking for a brain. Or mumsy dumb housewives, happy
little homemakers, washing the dirt till it's washing powder-
white. Or prancing, dancing, semi-naked nymphettes, who
you just know are there to titillate and then be attacked, you

just know are there to titillate and then be abused, you just know are there to titillate and then be raped or murdered or mutilated or vampire victims. And I wondered why that girl in the film was standing there screaming while her boyfriend battles with the intruder – screaming, you stupid cow, what's the point of that? Why don't you join in and help your boyfriend? Why don't you kick him, phone the police at least, why don't you hit him with that dirty great vase that's right by your elbow, you pathetic bitch – or you faint, you faint. He's chasing you, he's going to kill you, you're going to be murdered and you faint, you weak, pathetic girl, or you stumble, you stumble in those useless, impractical but highly fashionable slingback, peep-toe high heels – Oh God, women. What's the point of them, what earthly good do they do except get in the way, get under your feet, hold up the action with wet boring romance, whining on about how she can't live without him when everybody knows he's only got fifteen minutes to save the world. Or else she's whining and whinging about her bodily functions, getting pregnant every five minutes, nagging because her boyfriend's not paying her enough attention, or nagging because she's too bloody ugly to get herself a boyfriend, or nagging because she's got three kids and she can't cope, when everybody knows she's the one who wanted them in the first place, silly bitch, throw her a bunch of flowers she's so stupid she'll be happy with that, chuck her a box of chocolates that'll shut her up, take her for a meal that'll open her legs, pinch her bum that's a compliment, grab hold of her tits that's what she grew them for, walking around with great lumps of flesh hanging off her, going bobbity bobbity when she's running for a bus, with a cleavage down to her knees, with a low slung blouse and a skirt up to here, showing all her legs, tottering along, what's the point of it, what's she doing, showing everything, she's just asking for it all the time, walking round like a tart, she's just asking for it . . .

Slight pause to digest.

That's not me. I'm not like that. I'm only doing this so that I've got some friends, so that they don't think I'm a freak, so that I don't think I'm a freak, but I am one, I must be because I just feel worse, I feel stupid, I feel really silly dressed like this. I only did it because I was fed up being called 'ugly', but then I never particularly wanted to be pretty in the first place, and I certainly don't feel pretty dressed like this, and I only did it because I was lonely, but I've never felt lonelier than in this stupid dress and this stupid make up . . . so get it off me, take it off me (*Starts pulling off dress and tights.*) and if you want to call me a freak you can call me a freak because I don't care, can't be any worse, can't be any worse than that stuff, having to shut up and sit there and smile and try to look pretty for the boys, having to play sitting ducks, hoping to get lucky or something stupid like that. (*Puts on jeans from floor and shirt from desk.*) I'm sick of it, never wanted to be a girl in the first place, don't know how to be one anyway so why should I bother trying, it's stupid. (*Rubs on make-up remover from desk and rubs off with strips of toilet-roll pulled off earlier.*) Don't want to be thought of as a tart or a chick or a bird or a doll, a babe, a skirt, piece of crumpet, or even as a nice girl – even being a nice girl sounds horrible. Don't want to be thought of as someone you try to have it away with, as though you're going on safari or something, or someone who listens to you no matter how bloody boring you are. I'm not going to sit there, smiling and pretending I'm not as clever as you just because I'm supposed to want a boyfriend – I don't want a boyfriend. Well, not if he's just going round with a dress and a bit of make up on his arm I don't, it's stupid, it's pointless and it's not me.

Clean-faced, jeans, shirt and bare feet.

This is me. Dressing how I want to dress and thinking what I want to think. And I did it and it was fun. I still had friends, I was still popular, still went out, went dancing, and if there was a boy I danced with a boy, and if there was a girl I danced with a girl. If there was nobody I danced by myself . . .

Music: 'Power To the People' by John Lennon. Dances wild and abandoned, loving it. Music fades up and down between dialogue, dancing wildly in between.

I didn't care. I flung myself and I threw myself and my nails broke, my hair was all over the place, my clothes were a mess, my face was a mess and I didn't care. I just had so much energy. And my legs grew hair, my armpits grew hair, my eyebrows grew bushy – I thought I was turning into a werewolf . . .

Music.

And I interrupted and I argued and I questioned and I disagreed and I refused to pretend, refused to conform. And I refused to insult anybody by wearing this stuff (*Picks up dress disdainfully.*) because who's he going out with? That's not me – that's just a dress, he's going out with a dress, and I refused to insult myself by wearing this stuff, because I thoroughly believed it was this stuff's fault. Wearing this stuff is dangerous, wearing this stuff makes you wilt, makes it impossible to move, impossible to talk, impossible to think, impossible to breathe – this stuff just forces you to smile and panic at the same time. (*Throws dress down.*)

Music.

And my careers officer asked me what I wanted to be – I said John Lennon. She said, 'Yes, but how about nurse?' I said, 'Is there a skirt involved?' She said, 'Yes.' I said, 'No.' She said, 'How about secretary?' I said, 'Skirt?' She said, 'Yes.' I said 'No.' She thought I was stupid, but I thought she was because she was wearing the skirt and I wasn't.

Music – to end.

Pause, calms down, goes down, sits at desk.

There's something wrong with me. There's something seriously wrong with me. Everywhere I go girls my age are growing up, wanting to grow up. Going shopping, trying on clothes and enjoying it. Discussing make up, boyfriends and not getting bored. Talking about engagements, weddings, even discussing babies and looking forward to it. And me, there's something wrong with me because I can't even feel comfortable in dresses, skirts, anything that shows my legs . . . anything that makes me feel female – I don't know why. And my mum thinks I'm stupid because I've worn a skirt every school-day since I was five, and I say, 'I know, but it was different then, I had to. I want to grow up and make my own decisions, choose my own clothes, be my own person.' And my mum says, 'It's about time you grew up because you won't get a job in jeans, not one that's interesting anyway.' And I say, 'I don't care, I'd rather be a road sweeper than have to wear a dress!' And my mum says, 'Well, why for heaven's sake, what's the matter with you?' And I shut up and just give her a look, because I don't know why, I just feel like a freak. And my mum says 'Well, anyway you can't be a road sweeper that's a man's job'. And I go to interviews and interviews and interviews and finally slam out and go and buy a skirt because I'm begining to hate this world and I'm beginning to think I'm going mad.

Puts on skirt from desk and court shoes from floor.

My first job was with a very classy firm. Or so the personnel lady told me. 'Oh yes, we've got branches in America, you know, so we expect all our employees to dress accordingly.' I thought it was a bit like school, except that all the girls could wear anything they wanted to wear so long as their legs were on show, and all the boys could wear anything they wanted to wear so long as it was a shirt and tie and jacket and long ones down to here (*Ankles.*) and nice lace-up shiny shoes. And all the boys flirted with all the girls, and all the men flirted with all the girls, and all the girls did all day was talk about the boys and the men flirting with them, good or bad. I worked with two other girls and I knew I wasn't going to fit in the first time they took me to the canteen at lunchtime. They ordered *boeuf bourgignon* and I didn't know what it was so had a cheese sandwich and sat for an hour feeling intimidated and working class while they scoured the room hoping for a glimpse of Mr Banks from accounts because he was 'Really good-looking, and wouldn't you just love to melt

into his arms?' Well, no, I wouldn't actually. I was too busy
trying not to melt into the woodwork every time the boss was
around. He did nothing but shout all the time, horrible. He
had a very novel way of working, he'd scrawl a lot of words
onto one piece of paper, give it to me and I'd type the same
words onto another piece of paper – talk about trees. If I
couldn't work out what it said I'd go into his office and he'd
say, 'Why can't you work out what it says, do I have to be
interrupted every five minutes, what are we paying you for?'
And then I wouldn't bother going into his office, and then
he'd come out and say, 'What is this? This is rubbish, I never
wrote this, look that's suspend the account, not suspect the
account, you stupid girl!' And the other girls would laugh
quietly and pull faces behind my back because they were
friends and I wasn't, and I knew it was because of this skirt – I
felt embarrassed and intimidated and on show, I felt like a
sexual diversion for the men, all trying to get their leg over at
lunchtime or something, coming up close and putting their
arms round me, calling me 'darling' or 'love' and stuff with
their b.o. and bad breath. And they thought I was gormless
and thick, and I thought I'm becoming gormless and thick
and I thought I've got to do something about it otherwise
this skirt is going to make me burst into tears. And that's not
the sort of thing I like to do in public, and especially not in
front of those girls.

So being as this was a classy firm with branches in America I
went out and bought some culottes (*Puts on khaki-type colour
culottes from desk.*) because they're French and France is just as
classy as America, if not more so in my opinion. (*Discards skirt
on floor.*) And I wore them to work and nobody said anything,
nobody told me to go home and change, and I thought
'good', I thought I'm not going to play their game any more,
not going to be some tarty typist or a stupid secretary bird,
I'll play my own game, and I did, because I looked at myself
and I thought I look like a private, in the army, in Burma, yes
that's what I'll be and then they won't chat me up, but they
did. So I got some socks. (*Puts on knee-length socks from desk.*)
That's the game. I'm a private in the army in Burma and the

boss is a Sergeant Major, so of course he shouts, he's supposed to shout, it's his job, it's nothing personal. And the more he shouts the better soldier I become, I might even make corporal and then they won't chat me up, but they did. So I got some boots. (*Puts on 'army-type' boots from desk.*) Some big private-in-the-army-in-Burma boots and I thought they won't chat me up now, but they did, they just thought I was 'whacky', but I didn't care because I marched around all day looking efficient – I wasn't actually efficient, I just looked efficient and that's what counts in offices. And any time the boss shouted I'd just say, 'Yes, sir!' – and carry on marching. And any time they'd try to chat me up I'd just say, 'That contravenes regulations' – and carry on marching. I loved it because it was my game and the boss was playing my game, and he was playing it wonderfully, shouting away the way sergeant majors are supposed to, great, couldn't wait to get to work in the morning so that I could hear him shout and I could say, 'Yes, sir.' Felt so confident, so courageous. Ruined it though, got carried away, because he called me into his office one day and I marched in and said 'Yes, Sergeant Major, sir!' (*Salutes while saying it.*) . . . Embarrassing. Got court-martialled.

Kicks off shoes. Takes out trousers from desk.

Oh, well, Civvy Street then. Civvy Street and demob trousers. (*Puts on trousers over shorts and then flat school shoes from floor.*) Aren't they awful, aren't they horrible? Great, they won't chat me up in these and if there's one thing I've learned it's that I'm never going to wear a uniform again and certainly definitely never, ever, never a dress uniform because that's the worst, they're bad magic those things, it's true. That's why men aren't allowed to wear them, it's okay for half the population because they're only going to get married eventually anyway, but if everybody wore them the whole of society would fall apart, because everybody would be walking around being gormless and thick, and everybody would be looking at everybody else all the time to see what they've got on today, and everybody would feel embarrassed and intimidated and on show because everybody would be

looking at them and nobody would get any work done and
then where would we be? It's true. It's no wonder I never did
very well at school, I always thought it was the bloody
teachers – well, it was, but it was also the bloody skirt.

So there we are. I get myself a job at a place where they don't
mind trousers. Don't I look horrible? (*Gleeful.*) Don't I look
ugly? I get a job totting up numbers on an adding machine.
Well, it's easy, it isn't taxing and it certainly isn't classy,
thank God, since practically everybody eats cheese
sandwiches – *boeuf bourgignon*, just looked like meat stew to
me. Anyway this place is a lot better, there's a couple of girls
who spend the dinner-times plucking their eyebrows and
eulogising about their boyfriends, but I don't bother with
them, I spend more time with the older women because they
make me laugh talking about the smell of their husbands'
socks, or how impossible he finds it to hit the toilet bowl and
miss the carpet. And one woman tells us she's been married
for fifteen years but she hasn't a clue what her husband looks
like – he spends that much time in the pub, and we all laugh
because she seems to prefer it that way. And Beryl's got a
black eye – again. But nobody says anything even though
everybody likes her. And she helps Pattie pick out a dress
from *Bride* magazine, which I think is really odd but nobody
else seems to, nobody else says anything, so neither do I, just
keep myself to myself. And in between dinner-times I realise
I'm not working on an adding machine because that's
boring, that's a dead-end job, get trapped there, get into all
sorts of things you don't want to there, no I'm doing
something more interesting, more important – I'm working
on a decoding machine, yes that's it – there's a cold war
raging and MI6 need to know what those perishing Ruskies
are up to and I've got to give them the answer before half
past five. Yeah, that's an important job and I'm an
important person, though you wouldn't think so to look at
me on the bus, but that's the nature of things, I think Unsung
Hero is the phrase. And I like this job and I like these people
and I think I might stick it this time. Until I go into the stock-
room for more paper and the boss comes up behind me, puts

his arms round me and squeezes my tits . . . just for a lark, a bit of fun . . . and I think, 'I don't know what to do, what have you got to do?' I mean, don't I look ugly? Do I look as though I'm asking for it? But it was just a lark, a bit of fun. Spend the rest of the afternoon trying to work out what that's got to do with decoding for MI6 – realise nothing, so defect to the Russians.

Part Two

Music: – 'Over the Fields' by Soviet Army Ensemble. Enters wearing big khaki shirt and Russian-style cap over the shirt already on.

It's hard to get a job in Russia, everybody knows that. Especially if you're a resistance fighter. Packing cans in a factory might seem dull, boring and brain wasting, but I like it, I prefer it, gives me all day to think – and plan the revolution.

Besides, at the factory there's a girl from a different department, she says 'Hello' to me in the canteen every day. She looks for me, seeks me out, just to say 'Hello'. I feel pleased, and shy. She sits at a table nearer and nearer me every day. We both smile, we're both shy. I wonder if she's a resistance fighter. She comes in one day with her friend, I smile, she smiles back, her friend starts talking to her, I can't hear what they're saying but it looks serious and they keep looking over. She smiles less and less, and then she doesn't smile at all. They sit at the far end of the canteen. She ignores me after that. A couple of days later I leave my job because I realise I've turned into a freak – and I enjoy it.

I knew from the beginning that she thought I was a boy and I never did anything to correct her. In fact I went out of my way to make myself look more boyish. Did I fancy her? No, not really, it wasn't about that. She fancied me, that's what it was about. She made me feel good-looking, attractive, wanted, and I was myself, that's what it was about. She fancied me for what I was – till her friend put her straight of course which embarrassed and annoyed me. I don't care though, not that I care, because for years they've done it to me, individually and collectively, male and female, pushed and poked and backed me into a corner. Dictated what I can and can't do, what I should and shouldn't be. And me from four, from three, who knows, but I compromised, tried to

please them, do what came naturally but not try to question
their words, how could I at four, at three? And they told me:
'Little girls can't, little girls mustn't.' Mustn't climb trees,
can't have a gun, can't be Napoleon Solo or Illya Kuryakin,
or even Mr Waverly. Can't be Batman or Superman.
Mustn't rough and tumble and fight, can't get covered in
mud and grease and dirt. Little girls can't do what boys do,
little girls mustn't be like little boys. And they backed me
into a corner. Didn't have the ability then at four, at three, to
scream 'Liar', was confused, didn't understand, wanted to
climb trees, wanted to get dirty, wanted to rough and tumble
and fight. Was a small thing but was important at four. So
compromised, pretended, in my head. 'Be a boy' I said,
'Become a boy.' It was common, tomboy, hoyden, it's in the
dictionary, it happens a lot to little girls, brainwashing.
Brainwashing myself, subverting myself, turning myself into
a boy because little girls can't and little girls don't, but I
could and I did and I wanted to. So became a boy, then at
four, at three even. Felt confident then, could do it then,
could run and shout and climb and fight and not be afraid to
join in, not be afraid to test myself and explore the world.
And even then I saw it, even then at four, at three; fluffy little
pink things standing on the sidelines watching, waiting,
crying, clutching their dollies and being afraid. And they
were afraid because they couldn't practise, because little
girls can't practise, little girls don't practise, little girls
mustn't practise. Little girls can only stand on the sidelines
and watch. Practising only to grow older, to grow older and
stand on the sidelines and watch.

When I was a kid I was in the Brownies. (*Sing.*) 'We're the
ever helpful gnomes, helping others in their homes. We're
the fairies bright and gay, helping others every day.' (*Pause,
then sing again but with some venom.*) 'Here we are the sussed-out
elves, helping no one but ourselves.' I left the Brownies. I
wanted to be in the Cubs, the Cubs was good, the Cubs were
exciting, the Cubs were doing knots – Wow, knots! Later on I
tried the Guides, but left in disgust, they were doing knots, it
was so childish.

And then at five, at six, at primary school, being bullied and teased and picked on by the older kids, having my legs smacked by the teachers, being told to stand at the front, stand at the back, stand on the line by the teachers, being taught humiliation and degradation by the teachers – not to mention confusion as to where to stand. And I fought. I fought as Tom the boy, because little girls can't fight and little girls don't fight, and little boys mustn't hit little girls, but I was Tom and those boys saw me as Tom, they acknowledged me because they fought back, and we fought each other and taught each other as equals, as equal five-year-old boys. And other tomboys too, because I wasn't the only one, I wasn't alone, because as soon as a girl shows the slightest hint of spirit she gets labelled a tomboy, a boy, gets her femininity stripped away from her.

When I was about seven me and my friend Valerie were walking down the road one day when a man in a car pulled over, opened his passenger door and called us to him. And we thought, 'Oh, wow, this is exciting, this is an adventure, we've been warned about this sort of thing.' So we ran home and I told my mum, and she took me down to the police station to make a statement. It was really boring, there was no excitement, no action, nothing. I didn't even get to try on a helmet. And I thought if I'd had a gun I could have been the *Man from UNCLE*. If I had a rope I could have been Batman and lassooed him, Valerie could have been Robin if she'd wanted, I wouldn't have minded. If I had some steel tacks I could have been James Bond and thrown them in front of his car, so he'd have to escape on foot and me and Valerie could have rugby-tackled him to the ground and beaten him up, then had a Martini, shaken not stirred. Well, I didn't have a gun in those days but for the next week I never went anywhere without a piece of washing-line and a packet of drawing-pins. 'Dib, dib dib, be prepared' that's my motto. Unfortunately it didn't happen again.

And then at seven, at eight, my world growing. Looking around me and I saw Beatles, Rolling Stones, pop groups, gods, idols, objects of worship like Jesus. And I see they are

men, they are all men. I see men are worshipped, I see men
are idolised, I see men are gods, and I see Sandie Shaw and
Lulu. And I'm asked to choose a role model, a hero. And
Sandie Shaw and Lulu, they don't speak, they can't speak,
they can only sing and look pretty, look shyly at the camera
and smile and wear dresses, pretty dresses and pretty smiles.
But the Beatles speak, they're allowed to speak, they're
listened to. They're allowed a point of view, a sense of
humour, they're allowed personalities. And I think back, I
think back to Napoleon Solo and Illya Kuryakin and
Batman and Superman, and the Prisoner, and the Fugitive
and Doctor Who and the Saint and Man in a Suitcase and
Randall and Hopkirk Deceased and I'm beginning to learn,
I realise I have been learning from four, from three that the
only thing I can do, the only thing I can aim for, the only
thing that's accepted and applauded is manhood, is to be a
man. And I'm not. But I practise, I'm still allowed to be a
tomboy at seven, at eight. So the Beatles become my heroes,
the Beatles become my role models because at seven, at eight,
the Beatles are the most accepted and the most applauded
and I've got to aim high, I've got to aim the highest, because
I'm not really a man, I'm not really a boy, I'm only a
tomboy, which is only second best, but at least it's higher
than a fluffy pink little girl, at least it's higher than Sandie
Shaw and Lulu. And I become a Beatle fanatic, a Beatle
maniac, I eat, sleep, think, dream Beatles, I watch television
about Beatles, I read reports about Beatles and I realise I'm
not allowed to scream, I'm not allowed to faint, I'm not
allowed to cry and I'm not allowed to wet myself because
they laugh, it's laughed at the girls, the fans, it's scorned, it's
derided, the girls, the Beatle maniacs, but not the Beatles. So
I stop being a fan, I stop being a Beatle maniac and I become
a Beatle, I become John. I have a Beatle haircut and I wear
shorts at playtime, I'm forbidden trousers but I'm allowed
shorts at playtime and I see pictures of Beatles in shorts on
bubble-gum cards, so I compromise, I'm happy, I'm a Beatle
on a bubble-gum card, and sometimes I'm Paul, but mostly
I'm John and I continue to brainwash and I continue to
subvert because I don't want to be laughed at, I don't want

to be derided, I don't want to stand on the sidelines
humiliated and degraded and reduced to watching. I want
to join in, I've got energy.

One day I was sitting on the bus going to school and a fluffy
pink little girl was sitting opposite with her mummy on the
side seats. And she looked at me then said in a really loud
voice for the whole bus to hear, she said, 'Mummy, why is
that boy wearing a skirt?' And I looked at her, fluffy pink
little buck-toothed cry-baby, and I said in an equally loud
voice for the whole bus to hear, 'My dear girl, I am not a boy
– I am John Lennon!' That's told her I thought, and the rest
of the world come to that.

And at eleven, at twelve, it's big school. I go to big school and
learn needlework and cookery, and I wonder if John Lennon
can sew, and deep down I know he can't, but then I realise
that prisoners do, as a punishment in prison mail-bags are
sewn and that sounds interesting, that sounds heroic. So for
the next six years I'm a misguided armed robber from a
broken home, sewing mail-bags once a week. And I continue
to brainwash and I continue to subvert and once a week in
cookery I'm stuck, because I can't seem to connect this
activity, I can't find anything in it, I'm beginning to wonder
what's the point, it's so boring, till the cookery teacher
bounds in and says 'How to make pastry to be proud of' and
then it hits me, I realise I'm learning to cook for my future
husband, that's it, that's all, there's nothing else, that's my
life, learning to feed my future family. And I think this isn't
me, this isn't John, it isn't an armed robber, so I make my
stand, a silent protest, I forget my cookery basket. I can't
carry a cookery basket, I leave it at home, leave it at the bus
stop, leave it on the bus, throw it over a hedge, just get rid of
it, and as a punishment instead I'm forced to wash pans,
forced to wash pans with a scouring pad, and I think, good,
another six years of imprisonment and punishment and
heroics, thanks a lot, miss. And in big school I'm still
forbidden trousers, I'm still forced to wear easy access
clothing for the boys, but the problem isn't just knickers any
more it's the whole body, it's growing and sprouting things.

And in big school there is no playtime, there's only breaks
and dinner-times and shorts are forbidden, so the question
for the next six years is why is John Lennon wearing a skirt
for heaven's sake? And at eleven, at twelve, in big school
there's something else, now there's subtlety and an insidious
feeling that boys are getting proper education and I'm being
tolerated and boys are looking for careers and I'm passing
the time and boys are taken seriously and I'm a joke, and the
brainwashing comes thick and fast now, the subversion is
desperate because I realise I'm beginning to fade, I'm
ceasing to exist. And the class is asked what they want and
boys say 'Airline pilot' and girls say 'Air-hostess', and boys
say 'Doctor' and girls say 'Nurse', and boys say
'Management executive' and girls say 'Secretary'. And I,
John, and the other tomboys we just look, we just stare and
say nothing because there's nothing we can say, we haven't
even been included, because we've faded, we've ceased to
exist. And I look around me and I see no more Napoleon Solo
or Illya Kuryakin, no more Batman or Superman, no more
Beatles. I see only firsts and seconds and lines being drawn
and eyes being closed so I shut up about John Lennon. I shut
up but secretly I brainwash and secretly I subvert and I don't
know why any more but it's habit, and it seems somehow to
be a necessity and it seems somehow to be survival because I
can't help thinking that really I just don't want to be a
second-class girl.

*Music: 'Woman Is The Nigger Of The World' by John Lennon.
Striptease to music taking off bra first from under clothes, then
'Russian' and 'Burma' clothes – everything in fact except vest and
knickers, then takes jeans from desk and 'sexily' puts them on to music –
stripping off the hidden personality.*

(*Joyous.*) Women's lib, women's liberation, The Woman's
Liberation Movement. Oh wow, that's like the French
resistance, like freedom fighters, that's something heroic.
That's what I want, that's what I could do, fighting for
freedom, liberation, I could be a real hero. Women's lib . . .
there'd be espionage and sabotage, intrigue, excitement,
danger, running, lots of running and physical exertion,

physical sweat. I saw them on the telly, burning their bras, they were on the news, they're important, they were being interviewed. I don't know what they said but they don't wear dresses or skirts or make up or tights either, they're probably just like me, they probably hate being female too. But when we've all got together and fought a few battles, shown the world that we're not just silly little acquiescent china dolls, then we can start to like ourselves, start to realise that it's okay to be female, it's good to be female, that we can be girls and gutsy heroes at the same time. And I can do it then, I can stop brainwashing, stop subverting, I can be female and be proud, stop feeling ashamed, stop hiding, covering up, stop feeling second class, stop being a stupid boy. I can start to like myself, start to love myself, be myself. Women's lib it'll be great, it'll be like the Fab Four would have been if they hadn't started wearing those stupid tights.

We'll get motorbikes. We'll ride around in packs on motorbikes like hell's angels, looking scruffy but confident and in control, and we'll liberate women, we'll liberate girls . . . we'll liberate anyone, we don't mind, you want liberating, send for us. We'll start off with schools first, we'll go round to the board of governors and force them to change the rules about skirts, unless they can come up with a reasonable explanation as to why. Force them to put self-defence on the curriculum – ju-jitzu for girls only, instead of needlework, unless it's poison dart needlework of course, so that they can learn to defend themselves, fight back, and not have to worry about who's stronger or weaker or whatever, so they can learn to stand up for themselves and be confident, and boys and men will think twice about walking all over them, think twice about them being helpless victims. Then we'll go round offices, factories, workplaces and show women how to poke a pencil in the eye of sexual molesters – say, 'Do it with a smile, girls, you're good at that.' Then we'll steal the molesters' clothes, see how he copes walking around feeling naked and ashamed, trying to work while everybody's gawping at his body, I bet he'll feel gormless. We'll set up refuges for battered women, battered children, battered anybodies, they tell us who and we go round and batter the batterer. If he complains, says it's not fair because it's four against one, we'll say, 'We don't care, we're no longer going to be the fairer sex, pal!' Then we'll cheerfully duff him up, teach him a lesson. And on our days off we'll go round courtrooms and laugh and snigger at the judge in his stupid wig and stupid gown and we'll say 'Oi, darling, where'd you get your frock? You're asking for it wearing that frock aren't you, judgy wudgy baby?' And we'll go round publishing houses where they make girls' comics and women's magazines and we'll threaten to blow up the building unless they print stories and articles showing exciting and adventurous females, women being courageous, women being brave, saving the world and getting their man, so that people can say, 'Oh yeah, I want to be a woman's libber, that's more intersting than knitting patterns and beauty tips!' And as for programme makers and film makers who think it's titillating to show women looking attractive and desirable even while they're being raped or mutilated – we'll just shoot them – they can be the martyrs for the cause.

Meanwhile we'll ride around in packs on motorbikes, looking confident and strong and really good, so that young girls and teenagers can watch us riding past and say, 'Oh wow, I wanna be like that when I grow up!' And young boys and teenagers can watch us riding past and say, 'Oh yeah, that's my kind of girl, I wouldn't mind riding pillion with her!' Because we'll look so good, so special, and we'll be sexual, we'll be so sexual, not passive sexual, or romantic sexual, or dirty or virginal or ashamed, or doing it because he wants to do it, we'll do it because we want to do it, we'll stand on our motorbikes and do wheelies and shout, 'Yeah we're sexual, we feel horny too – right now in fact!' – that'll scare them. But we won't be tarts. We can't be tarts because we'll be in control, we'll have the power of our own bodies, they'll finally belong to us, so they can't call us tarts. And if they do we'll just duff them up, because we could do that too. But most of all it'll be fun, women's liberation is going to be such fun, we'll ride around together, laughing and giggling and showing the whole world how great it is to be female, how bloody marvellous it is to be female, when you're the sort of female you want to be and not what you're supposed to be or expected to be.

And then I went to a meeting. A women only group. And I said, 'Who's in charge?' and they said, 'We all are.' And they talked about sisterhood and patriarchy and politics – or more to the point, how they hated men. And I said, 'Doesn't anybody hate women? Doesn't anybody hate being a woman? Doesn't anybody hate being thought of as kind and gentle and understanding and supportive and patient and democratic and nurturing and reasonable and non-aggressive and helpful and self-sacrificing and fair-minded and co-operative? Doesn't anybody hate being thought of as nice? Like a biscuit? Doesn't anybody want to be a hero? Doesn't anybody just love what men do and want to do it too? Isn't there anybody here who's insanely jealous that they weren't born a boy? That they weren't born with the opportunity to do anything they wanted to do without having to apologise or justify or explain or feel guilty or awkward or feel like a freak or be ridiculed or persecuted or ostracised or wait till it's fashionable?' And they said, 'No.' And I said, 'What's wrong with me then, why am I such a freak? Why can't I just be a woman, what are you then?' And they said, 'Oppressed.' Fine. Be that then.

Sings while taking shirt out of desk, and putting it on to cover up breasts.

Sing if you're glad to be gay, sing if you're happy that way, hey.

Got a job in an arts centre, in the café cooking carrot cake. (I started that trend, only did it as a joke, didn't expect anybody to eat it!) Only applied for the job because everybody was wearing jeans, never once saw a leg the whole time I was there, thought I've got to fit in here, it's got to be here, there's nowhere else. Course, it was very middle class, very right on, crawling with feminists, having meetings, because everybody was in charge. (Can I move? – Can we

discuss it?) And while I was there I saw endless films, plays,
cabarets, bands, poets, meetings, discussions, conversations,
workshops, seminars, books, pamphlets, posters about
women and poverty, women and misogyny, women and
rape, women and violence, women and pornography,
women and sexuality, women and abortion, women and
fear, women and crime, women in the workplace, women in
the home, women with children, women without children,
women with men, women with women, women in isolation,
women in society, women being confused, women being
used, women being abused, women being refused, women
being repressed, women being suppressed, women being
oppressed, women being depressed, women wanting
equality, women wanting justice, women wanting freedom,
women wanting peace. And I got chatted up by a lesbian –
No, I'm a boy, you know. Got invited to women only
meetings by feminists – No, I'm a boy, you know. Got
coerced into a discussion about sexual politics and women's
problems by a right-on liberal man – I'm a boy, you know.
Got chatted up by a not so right-on liberal man – I'm a boy,
you know. I'm a boy. I'm not going to take any more of that
crap – I had energy. I'm a boy and I get annoyed at people
who assume otherwise, I get annoyed at people who think it's
a problem and want to put me straight, I get annoyed at
people who think I'm some kind of traitor to some kind of
Cause, I get annoyed at people who want to show me positive
images of women, thinking all I need to do is read a book
about goddesses and I'll be cured, I get annoyed at people
who think it's lack of confidence, lack of beauty, lack of a
boyfriend or lack of marbles, and I get raging at people who
think it's man-hating because that's less logical than me
saying I'm a boy in the first place. I'm a boy. I am. I ignore
all this (*Below the neck.*) stuff – it's too fat, it's too thin, it's too
tall, it's too short, too big, too small, not the right shape, the
right size, the right colour, the right look, it's a woman's
body, it's pathetic, I hate it, I want to hit it, want to beat it
up, want to cover it in bruises, want to mash it, want to rip it
up, want to disfigure it, want to destroy it, want to kill it, it's
weak, second rate, second class, second best, it's passive, it's

apologetic, it's guilt ridden, it gets blamed for everything,
has to fight for everything, fight itself, fight other people,
fight every day and never win, never be a hero, so what's the
point, keep it covered up and ignore it, pretend it doesn't
exist, stop fighting and have some fun.

Sing.

Sing if you're glad to be gay.

Met a lot of gays at the arts centre, funnily enough. I liked
them, got on with them, the only people I felt comfortable
with, the only people I could be myself with, because they
were the only people who didn't want me to be anything else.
Lesbians wanted me to be lesbian, feminists wanted me to be
feminist, feminines wanted me to be feminine, new liberal
man wanted me to have all the answers, old boy network
thought they had all the answers – gay men couldn't give a
toss.

Sing.

Sing if you're happy that way, hey.

I met a man in the café, well, he looked like a man, talked like
a man, walked like a man, only problem was he hated men. I
said, 'Are you gay, I thought you were gay?' He said, 'I don't
think so.' I said 'Well, what are you then?' He said, 'I don't
know.' I said, 'Welcome to the club.'

I said, 'Are you a woman?' He said, 'No.' I said, 'Do you like
women?' He said, 'Yes.' I said, 'What's the problem then?'
He said, 'Put a man and a woman together and you've
immediately got two conditioned, role-playing stereotypes,
reinforcing each other's myth.' I said, 'Are you a liberal?' He
said, 'Yes.' I said, 'Boy, have you got problems!' He said,
'What about you?' I said, 'Me? I'm a boy.' He said, 'Do you
think you might be gay?' I said, 'I might be.' He said, 'In that
case, I might be gay too.'

*Music: 'Strangers In The Night' by Frank Sinatra. Dances floaty,
romantically, a parody of being 'in love'. Music fades up and down
between dialogue, dancing more clichéd in between.*

We started as friends, talking, exploring, treading on each
other's toes, accusing each other of stereotyping, arguing
and questioning assumptions, sorting out what was wanted
with what was expected. And then we just invented
characters.

Music and dance.

Did he ever look at me, talk to me or think of me as female?
Yes. And did I shout, did I argue, did I fight, did I walk out,
did I tell him to get out, did I refuse to speak to him for hours,
days, weeks, months, till he rethought and reviewed the
situation? Yes. And did he put up with it? Yes he did, it's
what we both wanted, it's what we both agreed.

Music and dance.

I took a crash course in out-and-out manhood. And I found
the key. Society wanted me to be, and saw me as nothing
more, nothing else, nothing other, than breeding equipment,
a womb, a womb-man. Since four, since three, since birth
even, they wanted me to be the future. No career, no hobbies,
no brain, no mind, no thoughts other than the bearer of
mankind, the carrier of creation – and we laughed. And
every example we came up with, everything we talked
about, everywhere we went, everyone me met, we found a
sperm and an ovum at the bottom of it, and we thought it was
so weird, and so neurotic. Females from birth being trained
to be pretty, to be attractive, to look in the mirror and say
'that's all you've got', since two, since two years old, being
put into silly little dresses to make them aware of their cunts,
to make them focus on their cunts and know that's the most
important part of them – that's the only part of them, to
attract a man, attract a sperm – wiggle, wiggle, wiggle. A
lifelong career, like some travelling salewoman carying her
equipment in a suitcase for all to see. Always open for
business, always looking for that deal of a lifetime, that sale of
the century. Searching out the good sperm (hello, darling),
avoiding the bad sperm (keep your hands off me, you sticky,
drippy lecher), and keeping a polite but friendly distance
from indifferent sperm (you never know when you might

need them). Females from birth being trained to be passive, to be sedate, to smile and avoid danger and protect their wombs, avoid the danger of dropping their wombs. Get off the cricket pitch and go into the pavilion and make sandwiches, it's safer. Females from birth being trained to rely on men to protect them, men protecting them from unwanted sperm, men protecting them for their sperm, for their future – (*Like a nasty spider*.) Oh, my goodness – what's the matter, darling? – it's a sperm, it's a sperm – I'll get it, I'll get it, I'll get it, I got it, I got it, I got it – oh, thank you, darling – that's all right, (*Mimes male wanking*.) here have some good sperm, it's mine – oh, thank you, darling – that's okay, now go and make the tea. Females from birth being told 'Do whatever you want girls, but whatever you do don't loose your femininity' because femininity's just another word for fuckability and fuckability's just another word for future. And we stood on the sidelines of society like two gay men and we laughed – and then we looked up other words in the dictionary beginning with the letter 'F', because that's the kind of people we are.

Then we rearranged and changed the names of anatomy and found ambiguous positions and had sex. And it was wombless, to us in our heads. And it was also safe sex, because condoms are notoriously safe, to all those who don't use them.

And I went to the doctor and he found a lump in my stomach, a growth. Well, he called it a baby, but I called it a growth, because I couldn't accept that word, because if I accepted that word I'd have to accept everything I've fought against and everything I've laughed at, and I'd have to accept that it all made sense, it was all logical – conform or be persecuted, breed or piss off, and make sure that what you breed is the right colour and the right creed for your culture. And then I'd have to accept motherhood. I'd have to accept that I could only be a hero to myself, a silent, self-effacing hero only then, after nine months, then at the moment of birth, bang that's it, there's the heroics, that's all you can aspire to, and expect no acknowledgement from others

except perhaps a pat on the head and the words 'Good girl'
like an obedient dog. And then what? After that what?
Nothing. Nothing more than what every female's been
trained for; sacrifice, drudgery, being taken for granted,
being tired, being worn out, putting my life on hold, putting
my children first, loving them, watching them grow up,
reading about population explosions and worrying, feeling
guilty, trying to justify myself by being a better mother,
living my life through them, forgetting my ambitions,
compromising, hoping they realise theirs, if there's enough
room in the world by then, rearranging my priorities, saying,
'I haven't got time to think of myself, I haven't got time to do
what I want' and then waiting, growing old, watching them
leave home, hoping they love me, saying, 'Oh, well, it's
natural, it's what every woman wants – deep down, besides
there's nothing more important than bringing children up,'
and wondering why the world doesn't agree with me,
wondering why I feel less than second class, wondering why I
feel invisible and useless and bored and saying, 'Oh, well,
when the children leave home . . .' and then feeling guilty
for wanting a bit of time and a bit of peace for myself.

And I wanted it. I wanted that. My body told me I wanted it,
my own body winning when I thought I'd beaten everything
else, when I thought I was safe, when I thought nobody
could touch me, my own body jumps up, whacks me on the
head and says, 'It's time to grow up now and be a woman,
you can't be fourteen for ever you silly bitch.' And I wanted
it, I did. I wanted it and at the same time I didn't want it and
I felt it and I couldn't feel it because I didn't know what it
was I was wanting, I didn't know what it was I was feeling, I
didn't know if it was brainwashing or natural, if it was society
or myself, and I didn't want them to win, I did not want them
to win, I did not want them to brainwash me and subvert me
and shove me in a box labelled 'Womanhood' and slam the
lid on me. And I talked to my boyfriend and he said, 'A gay
boy, and he's pregnant, wow, what'll the church say, that's
really subversive!' And I laughed, but I knew it wasn't true. I
knew I'd buckle under and change, and I was scared to

buckle under and change, but he said it was up to me and it was. So I looked around me, and I saw women being told to be attractive, being told to be mothers and career women and homemakers and shoppers and lovers and wives. Women being told to have it all, and do it all. Being told to get to the top, and stay at the bottom. Be the boss, and clean the house. Women being told it's your decade, and your workload. Being told there's jobs for women, because there's no more immigrants and not enough kids. Being told you can do everything, and being told to prove everything. Being told it's your world, and being told to turn it. Being told you're in control now, you can do anything you want, but stay attractive and stay guilty and smile and watch the men because men are important, because men are the heroes and women can't be heroes. They can't be heroes because women have to sit there sedately, passively smiling and protecting their wombs, to attract a man, to attract a sperm to keep the world turning, to keep this stupid human race running, to keep providing the cultural cannon fodder. And I thought, 'No, I'm not going to play their games, I'd rather just drop my womb and be a boy, it's much more fun.'

Death and Dancing

Death and Dancing was first presented in Honolulu, Hawaii, on 10 July 1992, and subsequently at the Battersea Arts Centre, London, on 23 August 1992. The cast was as follows:

She   Claire Dowie
He   Mark Pinkosh

Directed by Colin Watkeys

Part One

'Don't Leave Me This Way' – Jimmy Somerville. A dimly lit disco.
He *dancing.* **She** *turns up, dancing. They spot each other.* **He** *makes the moves.* **She** *avoids them. Eventually, after some skirting around, they dance together, getting raunchier and raunchier till eventually* **He** *touches her groin and stops, surprised.*

They shake hands.

He   Hi, I'm Max.

She   Hi, I'm Max.

He (*to audience*)   That was how we met. A long time ago.
London University, England.

She (*to audience*)   That was his dad's idea.

He   My dad thought a son educated in London, England
would be a gold star on his resume as well as mine.

She   Isn't that pathetic?

He   Oh, give my dad a break.

She   Not him, you, wanting a gold star on your résumé.

He (*pause, nonplussed*)   Me I was gay.

She   He was gay.

He   Well, I am gay.

She   He is gay.

He   I came out from the word go.

She   What?

He   Well, the moment the plane touched English soil I was
out. But I wasn't just out, I was screaming.

She   Ow!

He   I was advertising.

She   Yoo hoo!

He   I was carrying billboards.

She   Thank you, Jesus.

He   Hallelujah! I would walk up to perfect strangers: Hi do you know me?

She   No.

He   Know who I am?

She   No.

He   Know what I'm about?

She   No.

He   Well, I'm gay!

She   Oh, yeuch – they get everywhere nowadays.

He   But then there was Max.

She   There was me.

He   She just kept popping up everywhere.

She   I just kept popping.

He   In the student bar.

She   Hey, Max, you know what? You've got to be fit to be gay. You have. Because all you've got is discos and marches. All this (*Dancing.*) just to get laid! And then there's the Gay Pride march. March! That means walking, you know. Why can't we sit in a pub and be proud?

He   In the refect . . .

She   March to the bar perhaps . . .

He   In the refect . . .

She   Better still, get a nice big diesel dyke to do the marching for you.

He   In the ref . . .

She   She could buy you a drink, chat you up, take you home, fiddle with your bits and you could still be proud.

Silence.

She Carry on, carry on.

He In the refectory:

She What do men do that women don't do?

He I don't know, what do men do that women don't do?

She They piss standing up. Right? Right?

He (*so?*) Right.

She Well, that's it. That's all. Don't you get it? It's amazing, I just worked it out.

He In the corridor: Hey, Max!

She What?

He How do you tell a gay man?

She I don't know, how do you tell a gay man?

He Well, no matter how big, how butch or how brawny – as soon as he sees another gay man he goes . . .

He/She (*together*) Yoo hoo!

He And then at a party:

She Hey, Max, give us a lift, now, I'm desperate.

He Oh, I'm sorry, I'm going in the opposite direction.

She I don't mind, just give me a lift, will you!

He Um, I can't, I'm going home with David.

She David. Oh, no, you're not.

He Oh, yes, I am.

She Oh, no, you're not.

He Oh, yes, I am.

She Well, not till he's finished . . . eating, you're not.

He What do you mean?

She Well, let's just say he's otherwise engaged . . . in the bedroom. Get my drift?

He   Yeah, I get your drift. Come on, let's go, let's go now. Bloody David.

She   He wasn't your type anyway . . .

He   Shut up! In the car. She's going through my glove compartment – would you stop that, you're so nosy!

She   Sorry.

He   You're moody tonight.

She   Yeah, well, that's Sandy. You know what she said? She said I was too aggressive, she said I was behaving like a man for God's sake.

He   Sandy? You're having a relationship with Sandy?

She   Well, I was. Not any more, God, that really annoys me, sooner or later everybody has to go and say that.

He   Say what?

She   They say, 'Why can't you be a bit more nurturing, why can't you be a bit more caring, why can't you be more womanly? When are you going to start using your womb?'

He   Ugh!

She   Yeah. I don't know any of that stuff for God's sake. I was brought up in a children's home. All I know is aggression and manipulation and selfishness and theft.

He   You were brought up in a children's home?

She   Yes I was.

He   Cool.

She   Yes it was actually. No member of staff staying long enough to bludgeon us with consistency. Or guilt. Or love.

He   So what? Did your parents die?

She   No. Well, my dad I don't know about, he was just a sperm in my mother's fallopians I think. But my mother's still alive somewhere.

He   So why did she give you up?

She   She didn't give me up! I wasn't given up thank you very much. I was stolen.

He   Stolen.

She   Stolen. I was ripped from my mother's bosom.

He   What like . . . (*Makes sound being torn away from breast.*)?

She   Yeah. Painful. I was teething at the time.

He   So why would they do that?

She   You know why they did that? They said that because she was a lesbian she was an unfit mother. Well, that's just stupid. Because everybody knows you've got to be fit to be gay.

He   Boy, that would piss me off.

She   Pissed me off. Pissed her off. Pissed everybody off apart from the social workers – who do they think they are, stealing children. Fascists. And they don't know what to do with them when they've got them, just shove them in a home . . .

He   Well, here we are, your place.

She   Oh, yes. So fancy a fuck?

He   No thanks, got to study.

She   Okay. Thanks for the lift.

He   She stole two cassettes and a packet of cigarettes out of my glove compartment, and I never even saw her do it! (*Pause.*) After that I started seeking her out more and more. Hey, Max! What sucks more, a gay man or a lesbian?

She   This place. Nothing sucks more than this place. All these student types walking around with books under their arms pretending to be intelligent.

He   Well, thanks for stepping on my joke.

She   Oh, I'm sorry.

He   Anyway. I've just been informed that I give the best blow job on the entire campus.

She   Oh, really? So you suck more than anybody then?

He   In a manner of speaking.

She   You want a competition?

He   No thank you.

She   Ah.

He   I really loved hanging round with Max. Because before, I'd just hang out with gay men – which is okay – I love bonding with my brothers. But there's always this one guy, you know the one I mean, he looks like he's flirting with you but he won't come right out and say it, makes you want to go: 'What? What? Do you want to fuck me or what?' But no, you can't say that, because then you're being brash and loud – you're being American. And it's the same with women. It is. Either that or: Hey, Max?

She   What?

He   Do you hate me?

She   Yeah, with a vengeance.

He   No, really.

She   No. Why should I hate you?

He   Well, I was just in the bar, and I went over to this group of women and I said, 'Could I use the ashtray?' And they stopped. And they glared. So I said, 'Could I use the ashtray please?' And they told me in no uncertain terms that I wasn't welcome. They said it was a man-free environment. One of them even muttered under her breath, 'You patronising, patri . . .

She   'archal, prick.'

He   Yes.

She   But did you get the ashtray?

He   They were scary, Max.

She   But did you get the ashtray?

He   No.

She   Well, why didn't you show them your tits? I have to.

He   Max and I started going places. Straight places.

She   Why did we go to straight places?

He   So you wouldn't bump into any of your 'wimmin' friends and I wouldn't bump into any of my boyfriends.

She   Oh, yeah. Not that we were doing anything under the carpet you understand.

He   Just wanted to be anonymous.

She   Didn't want anybody to cramp our style.

He   And it was great, wasn't it?

She   It was a laugh.

He   I loved it because everywhere we went people thought we were two gay guys. Although sometimes it really wore my ass paper-thin. For instance, we were in this one restaurant and we just couldn't get any service: 'Excuse me?'

Both clicking their fingers very camply.

It was obvious they weren't serving us because they thought we were gay.

She   Can't imagine why.

He   So finally Max had had enough, she just flashed her tits at the waiters . . .

She *does.*

He   That brought them running.

She   And coming.

He   Max, does it bother you getting mistaken for a boy all the time?

She   No, why should it, I used to be one.

He   A boy?

She   Yeah.

He   You used to be a boy?

She Yeah, when I was seven. Well, I thought I was turning into one, because I looked around me and I saw all these other little girls and they wore pigtails and fluffy pink dresses and they skipped. And I thought I'm not like that, I play football and I've got scabs on my knees and I'm thoroughly obnoxious – so I must be turning into a boy – because you would right?

He Well, you would – it's natural.

She I thought so. So I thought, what do boys do that girls don't do?

He I don't know.

She Yes you do.

He Oh, right, they piss standing up!

She Right. So I did. I went to the toilet. Imagine this, there's the toilet bowl, and I stood there like that – with my trousers round my ankles because I'm not stupid right? And I knew they held on to something – so I held onto my leg, thought it might be something to do with balance, because men do sway a lot, don't they? And then I pissed – all over the floor – completely missed the toilet bowl, just went everywhere. And I thought, oh well, that's what most men do, so that's all right. Then I waited till I was out of the toilet and half way across the room before I zipped up my flys – because most men do that too, don't they? Why? Why do men do that? Especially in pubs, in public, men everywhere, they come out of the gents, half way across the lounge and then they go – (*Pulling up zip.*) Why?

He They're saying, 'Look I did that without mummy helping me, I'm a big boy now.'

She Well, you don't get women coming out of the ladies going – (*Demonstrates pulling up knickers on the run.*)

He Around this time, my landlady started getting really narrow-minded. See, I'd met this guy . . .

She *makes faces.*

He   Beautiful guy . . .

She *throwing up.*

He   His name was Sven . . .

She   Sven. Sven, no vowels.

He   But plenty of consonants. Anyway, he had a few friends, you know how it is . . . and anyway . . . well, I offered to replace the carpet!

She   Why don't you stay at my place?

He   You sure I won't be in the way?

She   No, I've got a spare sofa, I never use it, and there's plenty of room.

He   Okay.

She   Okay. My place. My flat.

He   Wow, what a great place, How'd you get it?

She   I stole it.

He   You can't steal a whole flat, Max.

She   I can. I did. Well, it's social services, if you come from a children's home you can steal anything from them, they're a doddle.

He   Where'd you get all these clothes?

He/She   Stole them . . .

He   Yeah, I know. But, well, they're not exactly your style, are they?

She   They're for research purposes.

He   Research purposes. So what are you studying?

She   Life.

He   Nah, come on, what's your subject?

She   Oh, that. Religion.

He   What, you going to be a priest?

She   Yeah, that's what all the frocks are for.

He   Well, you're going to have to find yourself a choirboy.

She   What do you think you're doing here?

He   No, seriously. What do you want to be?

She   Oh, that. I'm going to be a guru.

He   A guru.

She   Yep. A guru. I got it all figured out during A levels right. I was doing Religion, English and Art – because they're the easiest right? Piece of piss those things, anybody can get them. But then it came to me – Religion to be a guru, English to be an articulate guru, and Art to design the posters – brilliant!

He   So we started to go everywhere together.

She   Not everywhere.

He   Yes we did.

She   Not Every Where!

He   Oh, right. Dates.

She   Didn't go on dates.

He   Liaisons. Good morning. Oh, excuse me, good afternoon, what time do you call this?

She   Oh, shut up, fuck off, go away.

He   You look tired.

She   I am tired. I met her at eight, we started fucking at quarter past – I've only just finished.

He   Boy, your tongue must be tired.

She   Whad dongue? I'm going to bed, I'm going to die.

He   Hey, hang on, don't you want to hear about my night?

She   Oh, yeah, what happened, what was it like?

He   It's amazing what you can do with a packet of crisps.

She   Huh? Go to bed! And occasionally . . .

He   Occasionally . . .

She Occasionally we popped in on the Lesbian and Gay Student Group.

He Just to say, 'Hi.'

He/She Yoo hoo!

He That led to some arguments.

She What a bunch of wankers!

He How can you say that? They're a group of concerned young lesbian and gay people trying to improve their community. They made some good points.

She Oh, yeah, like when Sandy said the world would be a better place if all men just fucked off.

He Well, she did have a point.

She You are a man.

He Oh, she wasn't talking about me, she was talking about straight men.

She (*tapping his head*) Hello? Is there anybody in there?

He Well, I think politics are important.

She Politics, important? Everybody telling you how to live your life and what to do?

He No, it's about setting a standard.

She Standard.

He A community standard.

She Oh, like all lesbians have to behave like this, and all gay men have to behave like that – like some sort of homogenous blob, with no individual . . .

He No, it's like what David said . . .

She David.

He He was making some good points if you'd bothered to listen to him, instead of making fun of the way he was dressed.

She Well.

He   It's about giving young people the freedom to be themselves.

She   Ha!

He   Giving them the opportunity to come out.

She   Like you came out, I suppose.

He   That's different.

She   Oh, why?

He   Because . . .

She   Huh? Why?

He   Well, you see, that's David's point again, because there was no support group when I wanted to come out to my parents so I couldn't.

She   Well, why do you need a support group – why couldn't your parents have supported you?

He   My parents love me.

She   Oh, they do, don't they? Your parents love you so much – so long as you do what they want you to do. Do you call that love? I call that blackmail myself.

He   You don't understand how small towns work.

She   Small towns. You couldn't give a toss about small towns. You could be gay in New York City and you still wouldn't tell your parents. Parents are fascists. They're shit heads basically. They bully you and manipulate you and terrorise you, and then they say they love you, just so you'll be how they want you to be, instead of being what you were born to be. And you fall for it, don't you? I bet you still haven't told them even now, and you're in London, for God's sake – small towns.

He   Parents. What the fuck do you know about parents? Your mother abandoned you when you were two years old, for God's sake!

She   She didn't abandon me.

He Oh, shut up!

She Well, I wasn't abandoned.

He *sulks.*

She Some people can't take a joke.

Pause.

(*Jocular.*) Most lesbians I know would rather tell their parents they were a psychopath – at least then there's a possibility of grandchildren.

He *laughs despite himself.*

She Mum?

He Huh?

She Mum?

He Oh. Yes, dear?

She Mum, I'm a lesbian.

He No you're not, you're a gemini.

She Mother, I'm trying to come out, it's difficult.

He Okay. What lesbian things have you done?

She Well, none, not yet.

He What lesbian places have you gone to?

She None, not yet.

He What lesbians have you slept with?

She None, not yet.

He Well, then, you're not a lesbian, are you?

She No, not yet!

He Okay, be a lesbian. Go and be a lesbian. I'll pack you some sandwiches. But make sure you fulfil your dreams. And fulfil our dreams – get married and have a few children first. Let your father proudly frog-march you down the aisle and I'll dab my eyes in joy at finally seeing you look beautiful in white silk and lace – instead of those horrible dungarees and hobnail boots which you insist on wearing. And of course we'll invite everybody who knows me, just to put an end to those nasty rumours. And then once you've raised a family you won't have time to think of such silly things as happiness – the valium will see to that.

She Stepford wives.

He Ah, I'm sorry, Max, I got a bit upset back then.

She No I am . . .

Start tentatively hitting each other, friendly like till . . .

He Bitch fight!

Slap away at each other.

She Anyway, you're right, I don't know anything about parents, I don't, but you should tell them though, you should come out to them. But you don't have to come right out, you don't have to hire a brass band or anything. Be subtle. Just tell them you're thinking of joining the navy – they'll get the message.

He In the middle of our first year we were hauled up before the Lesbian and Gay Student Group.

She Court-martialled.

He Grilled.

She Excommunicated.

He You're not really gay.

She Turning your back on the goddess.

He Why not get yourself a real boyfriend?

She Fraternising with the enemy.

He They just wanted to know if we did it.

She As if it makes any difference . . . What did David say we were?

He 'Gay identified androgynes.'

She What the fuck does that mean?

He   God knows. Nobody takes any notice of David, he's an asshole.

She   Well, you fancied him.

He   Well, he's a cute asshole.

She   Brainless but beautiful, just the way you like them. We should have stirred it up a bit, said something – yeah we did it.

He   Yeah we fucked – so? Does it threaten you? Huh? Man, woman, together, ugh scary. Well, we were being radical, we were being political . . .

She   We were drunk, sorry, just had one too many.

He   We were politically drunk . . .

She   Drunkenly political . . .

He   Oh, but it was scary, wasn't it?

She   Oh, it was weird.

He   Yeah. Because there was this penis running round the bed and we weren't too sure who it belonged to – Is that yours?

She   No, that's not mine, mine's bigger than that!

He   It's not working, Max.

She   What's not?

He   Men.

She   Ah.

He   I love men.

She   Yeah.

He   I mean, I really Love men.

She   Yeah.

He   But basically, they're not very nice.

She   Yeah.

He   You knew that?

She   I knew that. Have you thought about women at all?

He   Ugh, gross!

She   Ugh, women, nasty drippy things.

He   No, I mean it, I'm not joking, I'm really off men. I'm not going to any more pubs, clubs, I'm going to stay far away from the opera. I'm just going to stay home and study.

She   Study.

He   Yeah.

She   Why do you want to study?

He   So I can graduate.

She   Why do you want to graduate?

He   So I can get my degree.

She   Why do you want a degree?

He   So I can get a good job.

She   Why do you want a good job?

He   So I can earn lots of money.

She   Why do you want to earn lots of money?

He   So I can do what I want.

She   So what do you want to do?

He   I want to get laid.

She   Well, hang on, you got laid just this afternoon.

He   Oh, that doesn't count.

She   Why?

He   Don't ask.

She   Okay, I won't.

He   Just don't.

She   Okay.

He   Ask!

She   What happened? What was it like?

He   It was awful. We met on this train platform . . .

She   Train platform? What was it *Brief Encounter* revisited?

He   Very brief.

She   What were you, Trevor Howard?

He   Celia Johnson please.

She   But I thought she was a dyke?

He   So I'm standing there, minding my own business, then I see him – big beautiful man, big ole beefy man, the sort who could crack walnuts with his butt . . .

She   What an interesting hobby.

He   And he looks over . . . looks away . . . looks over again . . . looks away . . . then he sidles over and says out of the corner of his mouth, 'You wanna come back to my place?'

She (*mimicking*)   You wanna come back to my place?

He   So I said . . .

She   Yes, because you always do, so he said, 'Come on big boy' and back you go to his place.

He   But it was terrible, Max.

She   Why?

He   As soon as we were inside the door he takes off all his clothes, lies down and says, 'Do me!'

She (*lying down*)   Do me!

He   So I did him.

She   As you would.

He *mimics 'doing' her as though press-ups.*

She   God, you have got to be fit to be gay.

He   And then as soon as he's finished he says, 'I'm sorry I have an appointment, you'll have to go now.' I didn't even get a chance to get off.

She   Ah, shame. Still, never mind, you didn't miss much. I mean, orgasms, they're not all they're cracked up to be are they. People go on as though they were Tchaikovsky's 1812 or something, supposed to be all bells and fireworks and the French national anthem pounding through your body – they're not like that at all really. They're more like Old MacDonald really . . .

He   Old MacDonald?

She   Yeah, sort of E-yi, e-yi, Ohhh – and that's it.

He   Hum, you're lucky. All I ever get is E-yi.

She   Oh.

He   What am I doing wrong, Max?

She   Everything probably. Come on, let's find out.

He   Where we going?

She   Out. I bet I score more than you do.

He   And she did.

Both arguing at same time.

She   All I did was try to be a friend. I just thought go along, help out, see what you're doing – because I know it can be very intimidating going to a gay place on your own, nobody to talk to, not able to laugh, standing there with a drink in one hand, a cigarette in the other, feeling stupid, so I just thought . . .

He   Friend? How can you call yourself a friend when I can't move for you around my neck, how am I supposed to get anywhere? Nobody's going to come over, nobody's going to give me a second glance when they see you there. It's just ridiculous, I don't want to go out with you ever again.

She   Okay, fine!

He   Fine!

She   Fine!

He I'm sorry, Max, but everybody thought we were boyfriends. I mean, look at you, you look like a bull dyke.

She How can I be a bull dyke and a boyfriend at the same time? Anyway, if I look like a bull dyke, you look like a bull dyke, because look at us, we look the same.

He It's not working.

She What's not?

He Me.

She Oh, you. Well, okay, be someone else then.

He I can't do that.

She Yes you can, I do it all the time, just change your image . . . here, try these on.

He Leather boots? Oh, please. I can't wear these. (*Puts on.*)

She Just try them. (*Getting leather jacket.*)

He I can't wear that! (**She** *puts it on him.*) I'm Polish, you've got to be German to wear leather, got to be used to invading people.

She *looks him up and down, neither like the look,* **She** *takes off his jacket, takes off his T-shirt, puts jacket back on and sunglasses – very cool.*

He Oh, wow!

She You look good.

He How good?

She Very sexy. Walk around, let's look at you.

He *walks badly.*

She Not like that, you look like an advert for Preparation H, look confident, look tough . . . think lesbian!

He The only time I see lesbians is when they crowd round the bar, all elbows.

She Yeah, but they always manage to get a drink though, don't they? Come on, strut!

He Strut. Okay. Oh, I see, you've got to hit yourself in the dick every time you walk . . . ow, I don't think I'll last.

She That looks good, you look brilliant, come on, let's see how it works . . .

He (*reluctant*) Max . . .

She Come on, just be confident . . .

He Max . . .

She Remember to strut . . .

He Max, I appreciate it, I really do, but I think I'd like to try this on my own.

She On your own?

He Yeah.

She Oh.

He Is that okay?

She Oh yeah, fine. Well, I wasn't coming anyway, I was just showing you the door – no, you have fun, really, I don't mind.

He Okay, see you then.

She Yeah, have fun.

He stands at back.

She There are dark days. And sometimes the dark days turn into dark nights and you wake up in dark days again. And one thing leads to another each blacker than before till you swear that the blindness is permanent. But somewhere inside you, you hope to find the light switch, even though nine-tenths of you is saying there isn't one, and nine out of ten people are saying you aren't blind anyway. So you struggle in vain and in dark days. And all around the noise from the neighbours is deafening, increasing the isolation. Blind and deaf, deaf and blind, how to communicate, how to be part of things when you're blind and deaf. You can't see and you can't hear but someone, somewhere, out of the goodness of his heart is building wheelchair ramps. But don't complain, or you might be seen as ungrateful, even though in not complaining you are struck dumb. Blind, deaf and dumb. The year of the monkey.

She goes to back, takes off T-shirt and puts on leather jacket and sunglasses.

He (*coming forward*)   Wow, this is working, I feel really powerful. Everybody's looking at me. Nobody's talking to me but that's okay, I'm used to that, at least they're looking though. And some are sending beers over. All the big guys are acknowledging me as one of them. I feel so sexual.

She standing behind him. **He** *turns, looks, circles.*

He   I like your look.

They come together, almost kiss, till **He** *pushes her away.*

God, you're pathetic!

She   What?

He   What? Look! (*Her tits.*) You are pathetic, really pathetic!

She   I'm pathetic? I'm pathetic? That's good coming from you! Why? Because I don't have a cock? Because I haven't got the great god cock between my legs? Oh, that will never do, will it? Not in your world, not in the gay world where the cock is king. I'm not a man, I'm cockless, I'm a woman, well, how pathetic being a woman. Oh, or maybe I'm not being a proper woman? Is that it? Is that why I'm pathetic? Okay. I'll be a proper woman. (*Puts on long fancy dress.*) If that's what you think I should do I'll do it, I'll be a proper woman, I'll wear the costume, it's easy, anybody can be a woman. (*Stands in dress.*) Is that better? Less pathetic? I've just had a thought. Cock is king in the straight world too, isn't it? How weird, fancy having so much in common with the straight world. Oh, but hang on, because you're better than them, aren't you, because straight men they can push cockless people around, but then they say they love them, don't they, but you're better than that, you say right from the word go, you say 'I don't like cockless people, I only like cock' don't you, Mister Man? Do me up!

He   What?

She   Do me up! (*Dress zip.*) I've gone all weak.

He *does up zip.*

She   Okay, go on, push me now, go on, push me. (*She pushes him.*) Push me now, you leather queen!

He *backs off.*

She   What's the matter, do I remind you of your mother? Go on, you did it earlier, why not now, I'm the same person, I've just changed costume, that's all, so go on, why can't you? Why can't you push me now? Or maybe before, it was because you might just fancy me a little bit!

He   No!

She   Oh God, I fancy somebody without a cock, oh God a cockless person – and here am I supposed to be gay, well, what shall I do? I know, brilliant idea, I'll panic. I'll panic and push, push it away violently, call it pathetic and try to humiliate it. (*Yank off his leather jacket.*) Because God forbid you should do something that doesn't comply with your category, the little box you've shoved yourself into! (*Throw away jacket.*) Well, don't worry, it was just the image, it just fooled you, that's all, you're safe, you're secure, you're still gay, don't worry. (*Pull off his belt, throw it away. Start taking off his boots.*) Or did you really think you were tough? Hum? God, that's so typical. Gay men, straight men, you're all the same, aren't you? Give you an image and you believe it, start strutting around like little Hitlers, pushing aside anybody who doesn't fit, who's not quite right. (*Take off his jeans.*) Well, I have got as much right as you to wear that stuff. I've got more right, it's my stuff! So don't try that kind of thing with me, I don't like it, don't like anybody pushing me around. And I certainly don't like anybody pushing me around simply because they can't handle their own emotions! Especially not people who are supposed to be friends.

He (*standing just in underpants*)   We are friends.

She   Well, all right then, if we are friends, you can try on the power image if you want, (*Get long fancy dress.*) try on the control costume, but don't think it gives you any right to push around anybody who, in your opinion, doesn't fit, because I'll just push back. Okay, leather queen? (*Throws fancy dress in his face.*)

He   Have you finished?

She   No I haven't. Do you fancy me?

He   Will you take that off, you look ridiculous.

She   Do you fancy me?

He   No.

She   Did you fancy me when I was wearing a leather jacket?

He   Look, Max, I don't see what that's got . . .

She   Did you fancy me when I was wearing a leather jacket?

He   Yes.

She   Did you want to fuck me?

He   Yes.

She   Well, why didn't you?

He   Because I'm gay.

She   Because you're gay. So what does gay mean?

He   It means I'm a man who wants to have sex with other men.

She   I'm not a man.

He   Exactly. That's why I didn't.

She   But you wanted to though.

He   Yes.

She   Right, so put the dress on.

He   What, no!

She　Why not?

He　I'm not a transvestite.

She　Am I a transvestite?

He　No.

She　What's the difference?

He　You can do that stuff.

She　Why can I do that stuff?

He　It's acceptable.

She　To whom?

He　Look, Max, I don't like transvestites.

She　Okay. What's a transvestite?

He　A transvestite is a man who dresses in women's clothes.

She　What's a woman?

He　Oh, for God's sake.

She　Am I a woman?

He　I don't know what the fuck you are.

She　Well, why didn't you fuck me then?

He　Okay, you're a woman, are you happy now?

She　I'm a woman, okay, got that established. I'm a woman but you like me.

He　Yes.

She　You fancy me.

He　Not at the moment, no.

She　You fancied me when I was wearing a leather jacket.

He　Yes.

She　So I was a woman wearing a leather jacket.

He　Yes.

She　You were wearing a leather jacket too.

He   Yes.

She   We were dressed the same.

He   Yes.

She   So you were dressed like a woman.

He   No!

She   So you are a transvestite.

He   No!

She   Why not?

He   That's different.

She   Why is it different?

He   I don't know!

She   So put the dress on.

He   No!

She   Okay. All right. You are not a transvestite. You're not a transvestite because you don't like transvestites, because transvestites dress like women, and you don't like women you like men, so you say you're gay. But you like me and I'm not a man, you say I'm a woman, but you wanted to fuck me when we were dressed the same, so what does that make you?

He   Confused.

She   So put the dress on!

He   No, why?

She   To end the confusion.

He   How?

She   Well, maybe you're a lesbian, who knows? Just put it on, will you?

He   I don't want to.

She   Just for five minutes.

He   Not even for one minute.

She   Thirty seconds then, just try it.

He   No, I'm not going to.

She   What are you frightened of?

He   I'm not frightened of anything.

She   Well then, it's just a piece of material, you telling me you're frightened of a piece of material?

He   No I'm not.

She   It won't bite you.

He   I am not going to put it on!

She   God, you're pathetic!

Turns her back on him.

He (*sighs*)   Okay I'll put the damn thing on! There. (*Half on.*)

She   Oh, put it on properly.

He   I am, I'm choosing to wear it as a skirt.

She gives him a look, he reluctantly puts it on properly.

He   There, are you satisfied now?

She   No, I haven't done you up. So how does it feel?

He   Ridiculous.

She   You don't look ridiculous.

He   Don't I?

She   No. Actually, it suits you. You look better than I do. You look really good.

He   How good?

She   Very sexy, in a frilly kind of way.

He   Really? So am I the kind of woman you'd want to fuck?

She   What makes you say that?

He   Well, you're a lesbian.

She   I never said I was.

He   Yeah, but you sleep with women.

She Yeah, and sometimes I sleep with men, and sometimes I sleep alone. Sometimes I have a burrito for dinner, doesn't make me a Mexican. And no, you're not the sort of woman I'd want to fuck.

He No?

She No. You're not even the sort of man I'd want to fuck.

He No?

She No. You might be the sort of Max I'd want to fuck.

He Really?

She Maybe. If you weren't so obsessed with cocks and costumes.

Awkward pause. **He** *wanting to move about in dress, but not daring.*

She So how do you feel?

He There's a lot of air in here.

She Why don't you have a swish around, get used to it?

Music coming in – 'Never Can Say Goodbye' – as she backs away.

He A swish around.

She Yeah, you know.

He *floats around doing 'feminine' movements while* **She** *changes back into leather jacket, sunglasses and boots.*

He You know, Max, I always thought women did this kind of thing because they were women, but it's not, it's because of the clothes. Although I don't know why anyone would choose to wear clothes that make you do this kind of thing.

She Oh, come on, be honest, you're loving it.

He Yeah, I guess. It feels good.

He *floats some more before sitting on floor in a feminine way.* **She** *then circles round him, macho, hitting her 'dick' as* **She** *walks.*

She I like your look.

He *smiles.* **She** *kisses the top of his head.*

She   Do you get it now?

He   Yeah, I think I do. I'm sorry about before.

She   Are we still friends?

He   Yeah.

She   Well, that's okay then. Fine.

He   Fine. Hey, you got any other clothes I can try on?

She   God, loads. Listen, you help yourself and I'll go and find something special and we can really have some fun, okay?

He   Okay.

She *exits.* **He** *tries on a variety of dresses – expressing different characters to the music, till* **She** *comes back on in Marilyn Monroe type dress.*

He   God, look at you.

She   Look at you.

He   That's beautiful.

She   It's my special dress, you want to try it on? You can.

He   No, I couldn't wear something like that, makes me all hippy.

She *rolls her eyes.*

He   Hey, you know what we should do? We should go out like this, like two girls on the town.

She   What like laughing and screaming . . .

They do it.

He   Excuse us . . .

She   Got to go to the toilet, don't forget your bag!

He   Oh, my God . . .

She   Oh, I can't believe it.

He   Oh, my God . . .

She   He's gorgeous.

He   Oh my God . . .

She   He's lovely, I can't stop snogging.

He   Oh, my God . . .

She   I've got a rash all over my mouth but I don't care.

He   Oh, my God . . .

She   Hey, you're getting hysterical.

He   I know, I'm a teenage girl, I'm supposed to.

She   Oh right, carry on then.

He   Oh, my God . . . (*Notices suit.*) Oh, wow, look at that.

She   What?

He   Now this is my kind of man. Big, hunky, smart – and no head. Now this is what we should really do – I'll put this on and we'll go out like a 1950s couple.

She   Oh no.

He   Yeah, because it matches.

She   No, I'm not being straight.

He   No, not for real, just pretend.

She   I'm not being straight.

He   Just to take the piss out of.

She   Oh, you mean as a joke.

He   Yeah, not for real. I'll put this on and march in front totally ignoring you.

She   And I'll pull faces behind your back.

He   Like a real couple.

She   But not for real, just taking the piss.

He   Yeah, not for real.

She   Okay.

He *at back changes into suit.*

She   God, straight. Take my husband – please. I haven't
been straight for ages. I tried it once. I did try it once, lasted
about . . . oh . . . five minutes. I'd just broken up from my
girlfriend, who I really, really loved, and she really, really
loved me, and then she really, really didn't. And I was about
fifteen and devastated, because I thought it was me, thought
I wasn't normal, not right. Then I thought I've got to try to
be more girly, more feminine, like in a *Jackie* magazine. And
I didn't know how. That's when I saw this dress, that's why
it's special, was the first of my collection. I saw it in this
house, thought it was really feminine, the sort of thing
Marilyn Monroe would wear, and she's like the epitome of
femininity, so I thought if I've got that everything will be all
right. So I acquired it – as you do, in a not very ladylike
fashion I must admit but anyway . . . And I put it on. And I
didn't feel in the least bit feminine, not a bit girly, felt a bit
like a boy in drag really – and then I thought wait a minute,
because if I really did want to be like Marilyn Monroe I'd
have to grow my hair, and bleach it, and perm it and curler
it, and teasy wease it, and lacquer it. Then I'd have to pluck
my eyebrows into nice pencil-thin arcs. Or better still, get rid
of my eyebrows altogether and just draw pencil-thin arcs.
Then I'd have to stick all this different coloured goop all over
my face – different colour here (*Face.*), different colour here
(*Mouth.*), different colour here (*Eyes.*), different colour here
(*Cheek bones.*), remember my contours. Then I'd have to talk
like this (*Pouty and breathy.*), 'Hello, hello, how are you, so
pleased to meet you.' Like I was giving somebody a blow job
as I was talking. Which is weird really because if you talk to a
man like that, he answers like that (*Pushing the groin forward
and up.*), very strange. Then I'd have to stick things in here
(*Earrings.*) and stuff things down here (*Bust.*) like socks or
something – a couple of jumpers probably. Then I'd have to
shave all this (*Armpits.*) and all this (*Legs.*) and these side bits
here (*Edges of pubis.*) – not all of it though, mustn't shave all of
it, because that's tarty, just the edges, so that if anybody sees
you in your knickers, you haven't got pubic hair really. Then
you can drop your knickers and say, 'Whoo, there it is!' –
which is some sort of mating ritual, I believe. Then I'd have

to wear these stupid shoes which make me walk like this
(*Totter.*) and you can't run for a bus, well, you can but you'd
miss it so it's a complete waste of time, so you'd have to learn
to drive or find a rich boyfriend or something . . . and I
thought if that's being feminine it's a bit manufactured, isn't
it, a bit plastic. And then I thought so what is it about
Marilyn Monroe then, because she is beautiful. And then I
noticed it's her eyes. Her eyes are amazing. Her eyes scream
about her desperately unhappy childhood, completely
fucked up family and abandonment. And they scream about
this desperate, desperate, desperate urge she had to be loved
for herself – which was never fulfilled, because she took all
these appetite suppressants and then she died. So she had a
lovely waist but she was dead, rather a drastic way to slim I
think . . . So I thought if that's femininity; manufactured
plastic vulnerability, I thought stuff it, I'm more feminine – I
am, because I'm more natural – and if anybody says I'm not
I'll just kick them in the bollocks . . .

He *comes forward in suit.*

She   Oh, wow, look at you.

She *straightens his tie.*

He   I feel like a real businessman – excuse me, I think that's
my cellular phone.

She   You look really smart.

He   Hey, hey, hey, my pretty little thing. (*Lasciviously trying
to pinch her bum.*)

She   Don't you do that, you're not my boss!

Music: 'The Great Pretender'. They preen to the music, **She** *pouting
to him,* **He** *'answering' with his groin.*

He   You er . . . you wanna go out with me.

She   Go out? With you? Who's paying?

He   Er, I am.

She   Okay.

They dance to the music.

He   It was good.

She   We had a laugh.

He   It was fun. Come on, let's go out again.

She   Okay, what shall we do this time?

He   Er, I thought we could do the same thing again.

She   Ah no, not again, it'll get boring.

He   No it won't, we've barely explored it. Come on, it is just a costume.

She   Well, just one more time, but I don't want it becoming a habit.

He   It won't.

They dance again.

He   I'm really getting into this, it's so comfortable, nobody's saying anything, nobody giving us funny looks, it's all so effortless.

She   Well, it's all right, for five minutes. But do some people do this all the time? I couldn't do this all the time.

He   I could do this all the time.

Still dancing.

Max, you're leading again.

She (*annoyed*)   Sorry!

He *puts his arm round her neck,* **She** *pulls away.*

She   How do you tell a heterosexual couple?

He   I don't know, how?

She   No matter how short the man is, whenever he's out with his 'girlfriend' he goes like this: (*His head like rugby ball under her arm.*)

Exiting like that. **He** *pulls away and 'bows' her off first,* **She** *tutting, fed up.*

Part Two

Music: 'Mixed Up Confusion' – Bob Dylan. **He** *has books/papers.*

She   Why are you studying?

He   So I can graduate.

She   Why do you want to graduate?

He   So I can get a degree.

She   Why do you want a degree?

He   So I can get a good job.

She   Why do you want a good job?

He   So I can make lots of money.

She   Why do you want to make lots of money?

He   So I can do what I want to do.

She   So why don't you do what you want to do now, instead of doing what you've got to do to perhaps do what you want to do in the future. Because in the future you'll have probably forgotten what it was you wanted to do in the first place. (**She** *scatters his books/papers.*)

He   You're like a four-year-old sometimes.

He *attempts to retrieve papers.* **She** *dances round, scattering the papers further/generally being a nuisance. Finally* **He** *gives up.*

Will you stop behaving like a 'girl'?

She   I'm only behaving like a girl because you're behaving like a boy, and when you behave like a boy you force me to behave like a girl.

He   That's because you're forcing me to behave like a boy.

She   Exactly, will you stop it.

He   Will you stop having periods?

She   Will you stop growing facial hair?

He I will if you will.

She Have I? Where? How many?

He There, four. (**He** *gets up*.) Max, come on, we've got to study, finals are next week if I don't pass I'll have to go home.

She Don't you get it?

He Oh, don't start please.

She Okay, okay.

He I got it. Passed with flying colours, straight As. Max didn't even sit for her exams. I didn't go home that summer – 'Oh, I'm sorry, Mom, sorry, Dad, I'd love to come back, but next year's not going to be as easy as the first' – yeah, right! Summer was a blast.

She Summer was all right, but then school started again.

He It's not school, it's university.

She It's all school, haven't you noticed? The whole world's a school. Everybody running around wearing uniforms, terrified of punctuality and rules, while a few prefects march around making sure everybody does what they're told – does what the teachers at the top tell them to do. Government, it's just a big staffroom. The prime minister's just a headmistress. The church is a board of governors, the prefects, they're the police obviously. The army are truancy officers. Psychiatrists are careers advisors.

He Max, you're losing it.

She How can I be losing it when I've got nothing to lose? Nothing to lose, that's a marvellous state to be in – and of course sanity is the last thing on your mind. But if the lunatics are running the asylum, and the asylum's not your choice of venue, is sanity insanity by the madman's definition? Or is insanity sanity by the madman's definition? Whichever way you look at it it's always a madman who's defining, isn't it? And is it true that it only takes one man to see another man's sanity for the insane to become sane? So is it true then that it only takes one man to see another man's insanity for the sane to become insane? So is sanity just two people agreeing? And what's the likelihood of two insane people agreeing? And does it really matter when there's nothing to lose?

He Max, have you seen my project file? I left it here somewhere.

She How the fuck should I know where it is?

He But I need it, it's important.

She What is it, the gold star on the résumé, is it?

He Look, I need that project file!

She Well, it's got to be here somewhere.

He Well, I don't know how I'm supposed to find anything in this mess.

She Clean it up if it bothers you so much.

He Why don't you clean it up, more than half this mess is yours.

She It doesn't bother me.

He Well, it bothers me. And do you know what really bothers me? You sitting around on your ass all day! Some of us have got work to do.

She I'm working.

He Oh really, and what are you doing?

She I'm being a guru.

He Oh fine, great, well, you won't get far sitting like a bump on a log all day . . .

She Obviously.

He You should get out, do something, I don't know, go to Hyde Park, Speakers' Corner, convert people . . .

She Converting one is hard enough.

He Look, if you want to be a guru, fine. But you've got to get active. Why don't you write letters to newspapers, articles, start your own underground newspaper – I know, you could be a journalist!

She   God, that's so typically male, that is.

He   Oh, don't give me that, I'm tired of that argument 'you're so typically male'.

She   Well, listen to you, it's all man-speak.

He   You're sexist.

She   Okay, okay, society-speak then, it's all society-speak; getting a job, getting on the career ladder – changing society from within, how many times have I heard that one? Never met anybody who's done it, mind you. Seen a lot of people get changed by society, seen a lot of people become society but I've never actually met anyone who's changed society from within. Seen them obeying the rules, obeying orders – believing the orders, believing what they're told to believe . . .

He   Look, Max, if you ever want equality as a woman . . .

She   Excuse me, when did I ever say I wanted equality? Huh? When did I ever say I wanted to lower myself to your pathetic standard?

He   Oh, that's it! That's what I hate about women – you go on and on about what's wrong with the world, in other words what's wrong with men – when I was hanging out with the guys I didn't have to put up with this shit, just two men coming together, now that's equality, none of this superior goddess crap, none of this pulling out your cunt and waving it around whenever you were losing an argument . . .

She   Waving my cunt around? Oh, I like that, that's a good one, waving my cunt around.

He   Well, that's what you're doing.

She   Bollocks. I spend a year with you. A year trying to get to the point where what's between our legs doesn't matter, it shouldn't matter, should be what we are that counts. And we had a laugh, didn't we? The two of us, together? Taking the piss out of everybody, trying to squeeze themselves into categories? And we could have made it too, we could have finally reached that point where we could have been ourselves, I mean, it was within reach . . .

He   Yeah, well, maybe I don't want to do that any more.

She   No, why? Because it's not important now. We've got something far more important than our own lives now, we've got studying. Oh, whoopee! Studying is on the agenda. It's that time of our lives when we've got to do everything society tells us in order to be acceptable twenty years from now . . .

He   Will you shut the fuck up.

She   Our own lives, wants, needs, desires are now officially on hold, so let's start pretending again, shall we, let's start lying again.

He   I am not pretending, I am just trying to study, for God's sake.

She   Well, why? Because it's too much like hard work. Too much like hard work to listen to yourself – yourself, mind you – and know you agree. Know you are never going to be right, or true, or honest if you do that stuff.

He   I can be right and true and honest and still do this stuff.

She   Oh, you can, can you? You're righteous, are you?

He   No, I'm American, we know how to get things done.

She   Oh right. And when you're forty? Oh well, tough shit, wasn't your fault you weren't listening twenty years ago.

He   Have you finished now?

She   Yep.

He   Good.

She   Good.

He   Can I please go back to doing what I was doing?

She   Oh, by all means, be my guest.

He   Thank you so fucking much.

She You're so fucking welcome.

Pause while **He** *goes back to studying.* **She** *paces around.*

She Go back to wasting your life.

He I will.

She And wasting mine.

He You can always find something else to do.

She Or someone else to do it with.

He If that's what you want, fine.

Pause.

She I'll find someone who doesn't want to commit suicide. Find someone who's not going to be sidetracked by this studying malarkey. Find someone who's got the guts to stand up and be themselves for once instead of . . .

He For God's sake, will you just stop it?! Will you just stop . . . !

She Stop what? Stop what? Stop waving my cunt around?

He Yes!

She No! I'm not going to stop, I'm never going to stop, because that's what I am, it's what I always have been, that's me. It's me, that energy, you know that energy that we both have . . . well, we both had it, but you you're just sitting on it, but this is making me want to scream, want to explode – because you know what's happening, don't you, they're winning. They're forcing us to dampen it and stamp on it and harness it and . . . and . . . and worst of all force us to play the game. And look at you, you're doing it, you're playing the game!

He I am trying to!

She Well, why? Why? What's the point, this isn't you? Why are you doing it? It doesn't make sense. The only thing that makes sense is that I want to know who I am, and I thought you did too, that's why we got together . . .

He   I know who I am thank you, and I know you – all too well.

She   Oh, you do, do you?

He   Yes.

She   You know me, do you? Oh well, that's okay then, if you know me, I'm happy now, everything's fine, if you know me. Well, shall I tell you something? You don't know me, you've never known me. Every conversation has been a compromise, every meeting a waste of time, because you're just . . . people, that's all you are, people, and I hate people, I want to strangle people, running around, just trying to fit in all the time. But that's good, I like hating people, I love hating people, means I can go anywhere and do anything and nobody can touch me, nobody can come close . . . And you know what I'm talking about, that's what I hate about you . . .

He   I don't know what you're talking about, I think you're crazy . . .

She   You do. You know full well you weren't supposed to be labelled or gift-wrapped or boxed. You weren't even supposed to be labelled a man, look at you, just as you know I wasn't supposed to be labelled a woman . . .

He   No, I don't think, I know you're crazy.

She   But it's too difficult, isn't it – so much easier to pretend to want a career, so much easier to pretend to be gay, so much easier to pretend to be what your dad pretends to be I'll bet – well, not me, I never could pretend to be anything for very long.

He   You know your problem, Max? You want me to be like you and I'm not. I'm sorry I didn't come from a broken home, I'm sorry I didn't have to fend for myself from two years old, I'm sorry my parents had the audacity to love me, I'm sorry I can't hate the world and I'm sorry I can't rage with the same energy!

She   This energy. This energy that I was talking about, that you obviously weren't listening. This energy, that we both have, whether you like it or not, is too strong and too important to allow anybody to dampen it: not me, not some nebulous idea of a fucking family thank you very much, I don't know where that came from. And not you. And especially not you. And do you know why? Because I know you – when I was thirteen or fourteen I met you . . .

He   Oh, for fucks' sakes.

She   Yeah, Karen her name was. Karen. Exactly the same. You're just Karen. Because Karen and me, we were destined, we were meant. We were like that, you couldn't pull us apart – well, till we were fifteen that is, when Karen suddenly decided that society knew best. Karen suddenly decided she could ease and squeeze and fit – does that ring any bells? Huh? Easing and squeezing and fitting? So Karen suddenly decided she needed a boyfriend, to be acceptable to society, oh, she loved me more than anybody really, secretly, she told me just before she left, well, thanks, Karen, that's just what I wanted to hear. No, at fifteen she needed a boyfriend, a cock, to be acceptable, and I was cockless and therefore useless . . .

He   Well, maybe you just drove her up the wall, Max.

She   Well, maybe I did. Maybe I did. I loved her very much so . . . Maybe I'm doing the same thing to you, eh?

He *nods.*

She   Okay, fine, fine. Maybe that was the reason my mother gave too.

She *exits.*

He   She didn't come home that night. After a week I stopped looking. After a month I moved out of the flat. Did it bother me? Yes. But studying is great for taking your mind off things – and it gave me first class honours.

That was ten years ago. I never saw her again.

There are dark days. And sometimes the dark days turn into dark nights and you wake up in dark days again. And one thing leads to another each blacker than before till you swear that the blindness is permanent. But somewhere inside you, you hope to find the light switch, even though nine-tenths of you is saying there isn't one, and nine out of ten people are saying you aren't blind anyway. So you struggle in vain and in dark days. And all around the noise from the neighbours is deafening, increasing the isolation. Blind and deaf, deaf and blind, how to communicate, how to be part of things when you're blind and deaf. You can't see and you can't hear but someone, somewhere, out of the goodness of his heart is building wheelchair ramps. But don't complain, or you might be seen as ungrateful, even though in not complaining you are struck dumb. Blind, deaf and dumb. The year of the monkey.

When I finished college I went back to the States. At work I didn't tell them I was gay, not good for the job, the image, the career. But then in the late eighties it became fashionable – why every company had to have one. (*Buzz.*) Ms Jenkins, get me a homo, the ACLU's on my back, sure a dyke will do. Mind you, I'm not complaining I was going places, part of the new breed, me, three black men and four power-dressed women – all of us pretending to be white, middle class, heterosexual men. All of us believing the myth 'You could go far, it's great having someone like you on board, you've got the right stuff, kid'. None of us noticing the glass ceiling, not knowing that we'd be trapped in middle management, never going farther where we'd be a threat to the power keepers – the normal people. And I wasn't a threat. Around the office, office parties, functions, I was single. People talked about their wives, girlfriends, husbands – I wouldn't talk about my boyfriends because, well, basically, they weren't worth talking about, none of them lasted more than five minutes, it wasn't as though I was in love or anything. Then I met Simon.

I have woken up every day for the last eight months next to Simon. And I know what he's going to do, I know what he's going to say, I know how he's going to behave – and I know what he expects of me. Eight months. Constant, consistent. It's the longest so far, it's not perfect but it's the best for ten years. I want it to last, but it won't, never does. Simon's a nice guy, affable, easy going, gay, male – all the time. I said to him once, 'Simon, do you ever feel like being female?' He just looked at me and laughed, said, 'Yeah, what's the punchline?' But I've seen the female inside him, just snatches, hints, for a second. I think she should come out, I think he'd enjoy it – if he thought about it, if he understood. I broach the subject and we have discussions about queens, pseudo freudian analysis, mysogyny and mother fixations. I think, if he feels that way about the female side of himself (and myself), how am I going to get him to explore and understand the dominant, submissive, passive, active, childlike, old, frivolous, serious, up, down, extrovert, introvert, in, out, go with the flow, go with the mood, try it on and see if it fits, live a little, inconsistency that I feel, that I want. 'Don't change, don't be different, be like I met you, be like yesterday, I love you just the way you are.' I feel like I'm in a closet – half of me, half the time. 'Are you okay? You don't seem the same, not your usual self.'

I can't blame Simon really, it's me. I shouldn't live with him. Shouldn't live with anybody. Makes very little difference though, I'd only be out there all the time and no way can I be promiscuous, not in this day and age. So instead I'm getting used to biting my lip, holding my tongue and swallowing. Getting used to biting my lip, holding my tongue and swallowing as I sit round dinner tables with politically correct, liberal gays and lesbians and a few token understanding straights, discussing freedom – the freedom to be gay. The freedom to be yourself – so long as you are the same as your ghetto brothers and sisters – and the same as yesterday. In ten years I've piled silence on top of lip service on top of compromise and made it so easy to be secure and successful but so difficult to be myself. And why have I noticed? Because of Max.

I suppose, if I'm honest, she's always been at the back of my mind, like a nagging doubt. My trouble is I've always been able to cope, nothing's ever been that difficult, nothing's ever been impossible. But then my dad died. Three months short of retirement. Heart attack, massive, overwork and worry about the end of work. His retirement was all he ever worked for. His goal was that time when he could let go and do exactly what he wanted to do, exactly what he'd always planned to do, he could finally be himself. He never made it. Three months short.

So why did I study? So I could graduate. Why did I want to graduate? To get a degree. Why did I want a degree? To get a good job. Why did I want a good job? To earn lots of money. Why did I want lots of money? So I could earn more money, more and more money. Because when I had money things would be different, when I had money I could be myself, when I had money I could do what I want, when I had money I could die three months short of doing what I want.

Max was right. No, Max was wrong. It has nothing to do with sexuality.

My dad's funeral was awful, sickening, numb. Simon looked beautiful in black. I carried a nagging resentment of that all the way through the service. Wanted to grab him, wanted to rip his beautiful black suit off him, wanted to scream, 'Don't stand there looking like a beautiful successful businessman – my dad's just died from being a successful businessman – would you smoke if he died from cancer?' And then I noticed I was wearing a beautiful black suit too. What am I doing? What the hell am I doing? I enjoy work but look forward to the weekends, enjoy the weekends, but look forward to a vacation, enjoy a vacation but think next year's will be better. And I bought an apartment, it wasn't big enough so moved on to another, then bought a house, still not big enough. Got to work more to buy more, buy more stuff, because eventually I will buy right, eventually I will buy what I need.

The only time I felt real was at college, with her. What did she want me to do? What did she want me to be? And since then what?

I came back to England for another funeral, David's, the cute asshole. Two funerals in two months, makes you feel old – and David was the same age as me. He wasn't a particularly close friend, I hardly knew him, but it was the excuse, and she came to mind. I knew she wouldn't be there, of course, knew she was long gone. But the idea of England and college, a reason to come, memories of the past – Max.

At David's funeral I went through the motions. Scanned the faces, said, 'Hi, how you doing?' and pretended to be interested. Played the How Successful Did You Become game, where you manoeuvre and allow yourself to be manoeuvred into dropping annual salary into the conversation, bumping it up by a few grand because everybody else did and that's the rule. One upped and name dropped and surreptiously bitched and modestly crowed and acted sincere and appeared the winner and felt quietly sick to my stomach. Had she been there she'd have laughed at us. Performing monkeys dancing to the group tune. She always laughed. Not obviously, not blatant scorn, just a slight knowing grin as she stood on the edge of the crowd. I stood slap in the middle of them, smiling, monkey dancing, feeling sick – and tried not to appear too excited when Sandy said she'd seen her. Where, Sandy, where? Played the hypocrite, nodding in agreement as Sandy said she'd felt so sorry for her, given her a couple of quid, obviously penniless. Where did you see her, Sandy? Played the hypocrite as Sandy explained how she'd said nothing and walked away quickly for fear of embarrassing her. Give me a hint, when? Where were you at the time? Played the hypocrite as I disguised elation for shock and pumped Sandy for information, for clues, like an outraged liberal instead of excited, excited, elated and optimistic.

It was a great funeral. It was a brilliant funeral. I don't think I thought about David once. She was getting nearer, I could feel it. Sandy said she seemed homeless, penniless, possibly even mentally ill. I thought about feeling sorry, but for some reason I didn't, for some reason I was glad, for some reason it was what I was expecting.

After the funeral, at David's mom's, everybody gathered, memories and still more bitching. No mention of David except in mom's earshot. Finally I couldn't bear it any longer. 'Sandy, where did you say you saw her?' Speakers' Corner – of course! But she wasn't speaking? Wasn't ranting? Just listening? And then Pete said he saw her at a comedy gig. But she wasn't performing? Wasn't heckling? Just listening? Well, how was she? What's she like? How'd she turn out?

I looked for her. First Sunday. Speakers' Corner. Come on, Max. Nothing. Okay, I've got a week. I'll check out all the cabarets, comedy clubs, fringe theatre (I hate fringe theatre) – nothing. Second Sunday. Speakers' Corner. Come on, Max. I'm supposed to go back, my time's up. I'll just have to extend my trip – they'll understand, Simon will understand, they'll have to understand. Phone directory, voters' registration, why didn't I think of that before. Of course she's not listed, well, she wouldn't be, would she? Third Sunday. Speakers' Corner. Okay, go all out. I'll go to every gay and lesbian group, every underground political meeting, every forum – in desperation I even checked out the women's groups – it's a long shot but what the hell. Fourth Sunday. Speakers' Corner . . .

She   Well, I can see your hypocrisy and decadence from here. Your spoilt little rich kids' complaints, your . . . what's the expression? You've made your bed and now it's lumpy? Some people don't have the luxury of your problems. People are dying, starving, being tortured because of us, how the hell do you sleep at night? Valium, is it? Sleeping pills? What do herbalists do? What's the holistic approach? Anyway enough chitchat. What jobs do you do? What careers are you successful at? Who are you exploiting? Which people are you turning into slaves? Who are you helping starve today? Which repressive, Third World regime are you helping prop

up? Because we are, I don't need to know, don't need to be
told, because I know that anything we do, anything
involving a wage packet means someone somewhere is being
exploited, someone somewhere is starving, someone
somewhere is being tortured, someone somewhere is
needlessly dying. Oh, but wait a minute because I bet you
gave to Band Aid, so that's all right. I bet it was some poor
starving Third World slave who made the pen for you to sign
the cheque with. Or was it a credit card? Was it one of those
itsy bitsy, teensy weensy little bits of plastic that ensures we
stay forever in debt? Forever having to work to pay off our
debt? Forever having to lie and pretend and wear a mask and
a costume in order to work to pay off our debt? The mask and
the costume of the comfortable slave? The comfortable slave
with a house full of emblems of so-called success? Useless
trinkets and time-saving gadgets, because our time's been
stolen into slavery in order to pay for the time-saving gadgets
and useless trinkets. God, life's a bitch, isn't it? But what's the
alternative? What's the alternative to making money? Do
you know? Do you care? Is there one? Is there one when
every revolution that's ever been or ever been talked about
has been an economic one? Is there any way of ever getting
off this money-making merry go round and . . . oh, wait a
minute, I lied. I lied. There was a revolution once that wasn't
economic. There was a sexual revolution, wasn't there?
Wow, that was good. Didn't we have some freedom? We had
the freedom to . . . to . . . go on the Pill – and get the clap!
Brilliant. And then there was a women's revolution, God,
there's revolutions coming out of the woodwork when I think
about it. The women's revolution – 'Excuse me, could we
have an orgasm please? Thank you. Now could we have a
crèche?' But I mustn't take the piss, mustn't, because we
tried, didn't we? At least we tried. But how could we do
anything when we're all walking round with our tight cunts
and penises with knots in them? Because sexually, they make
sure we're so well-controlled, don't they? They make sure
we're so well-conformed, don't they? Whoever 'they' are. I
don't know. I think 'they' might be us. But I don't want to
think about that because it's too frightening. Not that it

matters anyway because we don't count. We don't. Not one of us, not one single human being on the whole planet counts, not one. Oh, the position counts – the position is incredibly important. Take the pope. Now there's a good job, isn't it, being a pope. But if the pope dies. We just get another one. Position filled. Fuck him he's dead, he don't count, can't even remember his name. If the queen dies, long live the king, so she don't count. So if they don't count, what hope is there for us peasants? There isn't one, we just don't count at all, we are just shit on the shoe of life. No, that's not true. We do count. We do. We're very important we are. We count, because we're doing it for – our kids! We are doing it for our kids. Yes. We'll teach them to be non-sexist and non-racist and all that malarkey – we'll beat it into them if necessary – and then they'll grow up and they'll change the world, they'll have the revolution, they'll grow up and they'll be doing it for – their kids. Oh. Well sooner or later somebody will start a revolution because . . .

He   Max!

She   Well, maybe there'll be too many kids in the world, I dunno . . .

He   Max!

She   What? What do you want? Interrupting me, I was on a roll. I was just telling these good people how fucked up the world was, I think they were agreeing, we were having a laugh. What? What do you want? Want me to help? Want me to sort it out? Must be something desperate you've been skulking around for weeks. I've been watching you.

He   Have you?

She   Well, watching, avoiding more like. Look at you, why should I bother? You're worse than everybody else and that's what pisses me off, because you know it's a lie . . . well, you knew . . . But that's not very nice, is it? Where's my manners . . . How are you? What you been doing? Making lots and lots of money I'll bet, yes, I can see you have and when anybody asks I bet you say, 'Me? I'm fine, I'm great, I'm a

fucking success with my bank balance, what do you expect?'
So not only are you a liar but you're also a hypocrite,
perpetuating the myth that you're having a better time of it
because you haven't the guts to admit you're stupid, haven't
the balls to admit you've been fooled. So how are you? Well,
do you know who you are? Do you know what you want? No,
of course not, how could you? You've just dived into the shit
and now you're swimming in it and wondering why aren't
you? And do you know what else you've done? Wearing this
suit, conforming to conformity, you know what you've done?
You've created more shit, more and more shit to just dump
over everyone else, making it more likely they'll drown if
they were thinking of swimming against the tide, no, no, if
they were just thinking of thinking, because God forbid
people should be allowed to think on this planet, all of us in
our strait-jackets – talk about wheel-clamps. Why don't you
shout about it? Go on, I'd have a slight nod of respect for you
then. But you don't, do you? Well, I can see you don't, I can
see you're keeping yourself so well hidden, just in case, in case
of what? Why are you doing this? I bet you haven't even got
any kids so what's the point? This isn't you. Go on shout
about it. Go on. Stand up there, on that box, in your suit,
wave your bank balance in the air and shout 'It sucks!' Go
on. Shout 'I'm a fake and a loser, I've wasted my whole
fucking life! I'm a murderer and a suicide . . .' Why are you
laughing?

He Because, Max . . .

She Don't laugh at me, pal, just don't. I'm being serious,
you only had one life and you wasted it – puff! I don't think
that's funny.

He Why don't you just say what you want to say?

She Say what I want to say? You want me to say what I
want to say?

Starts punching him.

You really want me to say what I really want to say?

Punching more and more till **He** *grabs and hugs her,* **She** *fights him off.*

Don't . . . ! I wanted a family. That's all. I don't care about anything else or anyone else. I just wanted one person. Just one who was of my tribe, who didn't think I was mad, who understood me. Just one, because I can't do it on my own. I see everybody and they know it's a lie, they all know it's a lie, but they just say, 'Oh well, that's life!' They say. And it's not, I can't see it, I can't do it, it's death, it's like crawling to death, and I just wanted one person to be with . . .

He   Well, you've found one, Max.

She   Who felt the same, who could see it and couldn't play it either, who wanted to play their own game, try and be themselves . . .

He   You've found one.

She   Who didn't want to be shoved in a box, told how to be or who to be, just one person with me, so together we could . . .

He   But, Max, you've found one!

She   So why did you study?

He   It was expected.

She   Why did you graduate?

He   I'd been trained.

She   Why did you get a degree?

He   For my dad.

She   Why did you get a good job?

He   So I could be like my dad.

She   Looks like you succeeded.

He   In spades.

She   Why did you earn lots and lots of money?

He   To be accepted.

She   I accepted you. I accepted you without any of that shit. I accepted you for what you were and what you wanted to be.

He   I know. That's because you're my family.

She   Was. Thought I was.

He   Could still be.

She   You think so? Huh? You think so do you? You hotshot, white, male, middle class, gay, yuppie, businessman, tosser? You really think it's that easy, do you? Just to come sliding back in? Think I'll run at you with open arms? Ugh, that's what I hate about you, what I've always hated, you think everything's so easy, don't you?

He   No.

She   Everything's so comfortable with you, isn't it? I bet your boyfriend's beautiful, I bet your world's beautiful. Well, shall I tell you something? The gay world sucks! You're so . . . so . . .

He   Smug?

She   Smug. You're so smug, you are, thinking you're above everybody else or apart from everybody else, well, you're not, you hear me, you're not!

He   I know.

She   You could have been, you could have been beautiful, but no, you just slotted yourselves into the straight world.

He   You're right, it's disgusting.

She   Just flipped a coin, that's all you've done, flipped a coin.

He   Only halfway out.

She   Why stop at who you have sex with? Huh? Why? Good start, shows your determination but why stop there? Why not look around, see the rest of it, why don't you reject that too?

He   Should reject everything in the so-called normal world.

She   There's no such thing as normal.

He   You're right, it's anything but. It's

He/She   Not natural.

She   Everybody's mad, they're all fucked, all running around like headless chickens. Supposed to have all this intelligence, all this knowledge, they call it the age of enlightenment, but oh God, the peasants are in danger of learning something about themselves so let's throw them off track by talking about cholesterol – and people fall for it, that's fucked, everybody's fucked.

He   Including us.

She   Yeah, including us, that's what pisses me off the most. So do something about it, get angry.

He   I am, I'm furious.

She   Well, show it then.

He   How?

She   Just get angry.

He   How?

She   Shout.

He   I don't know how to.

She   Just open your mouth and rant.

He   About what?

She   Whatever it is.

He   I don't know what it is.

She   Well, however it feels.

He   I don't know how it feels.

She   Then obviously you don't feel it.

He   I do, I do.

She   Feel what?

He   I feel, I feel . . . it's all in here.

She   What's all in here?

He   Everything. I don't know.

She   So what does that feel like?

He   What?

She   Not knowing. What does not knowing feel like?

He   I don't know. Feels like nothing.

She   What does nothing feel like?

He   How can I tell you what nothing feels like?

She   Try.

He   Doesn't make sense.

She   What doesn't?

He   You. You're confusing me.

She   What does confusion feel like?

He   Oh, Max, stop it. I don't know.

She   What does I don't know feel like?

He   I don't know! Okay! I just don't know! Why can't you accept that? Why can't you accept that I don't know how to start, that I can't rage like you, I don't have the ability. I have the feelings, yes, but I can't let them out, I just can't, I don't know how. And you, you make me so mad, because you don't see how easy it is for you. You never had to choose, never had anybody to please, nobody else's agenda to live up to, no family, no pressure, no confusion. I don't know who I am, Max, I just don't know! So don't tell me to just get angry because I am! But . . . you don't know what numbness feels like, you have no idea what pretence is, that feeling that one day, please, God, it'll click, one day it'll feel real, that feeling in here, nagging, clawing at me and I don't know what it is, so I can't say. How can I say when I don't know? How can I explain? So don't tell me to get angry about it, Max, because I don't know what 'it' is – I just don't know.

She   Well, neither do I. But I can still shout, can't I? It's just fun – that's all.

He   Well, okay. Fine.

She   Fine.

He   Fine. (*Pause.*) Nice jacket.

She   I stole it.

He   Some things never change.

She   Wanna try it on?

They swap jackets.

He   So do you fancy a fuck?

She   No thanks. I've got to study.

Drag Act

Drag Act was commissioned and first presented by Gay Sweatshop at the Grand Theatre, Blackpool, on 22 January 1993, and subsequently at the Drill Hall, London.

Performed by Stacey Charlesworth and Robert Hale
Directed by James Neale-Kennerley

Music: 'Girls Just Want to have Fun'.

A mannequin divinely dressed and coiffed – the sort of frock worn only by drag artists . . . or Barbara Cartland.

Rose *enters dressed in typical butch dyke fashion – over the top bump and grind and lip synch for a couple of minutes. She changes into drag throughout the course of the play.*

Mother would've been proud, she always wanted me to be glamorous. That's where she went wrong, I reckon, trying to get me to be all girly and feminine:

'Sit with your legs together, Rose, it's so unladylike to sprawl.'

Had she said:

'Look upon it as drag' it might've been easier – we could've argued about dressing down rather than dressing up – much more fun. I could've said:

'But, Mother, what's wrong with four-foot turquoise peacock feathers cascading out of my bouffant? It is speech day after all, and if that's not a speech then at least it's a statement.'

School speech day, learning how to curtsy, I never thought it would come in useful. School was the worst – we had to wear berets in those days and white gloves – cooking was the main thing – cooking and needlework and learning how clever men were, well, except Florence Nightingale – and she was ony included as an example to us all with her caring and nursing skills – and all my classmates insisted on stuffing their bras, so they must have taken it seriously, such is life.

But where were the other two, that's what I want to know. If at least one out of ten is lesbian – well, there were thirty girls in my class – where were the other two? Having a very, very private love affair I reckon, not telling me because of the messiness of triangular jealousies. And I don't know why people complained about forty in a class, at least that's a lover each and a nice four for tennis.

But I digress. I was talking about Mother – she's dead now, pity. Still she never understood. Well, neither did I till recently. I'm fifty-two years old and I've only just started living – I mean Really Living. Her name's Sarah, she's only twenty-five. Age gap? I don't care, think what you like. I've had fifty-two years of caring – fifty-two years of being told what is, what isn't, what should be, what shouldn't be – should lesbians be butch or shouldn't they be more womanly? (Whatever that means!) That was somewhere around the eighties, a terrible decade.

I'd just broken up with Jackie, my lifelong lover of fifteen years, when I got into a hell of an argument with some jumped-up little dyke. Well, I say dyke, I reckon she was one of those 'Sleeping with women is a political statement' types – in other words heterosexual but experimenting. She was blethering on that lesbians shouldn't look like lesbians, she said it's more political to look feminine and that butch dykes were simply strutting around wearing the symbols of male oppression and patriarchy.

I told her, I said:

'I was a lesbian before you were born, madam, and as far as I'm aware I've never strutted in my life, let alone oppressed anybody, so don't tell me!'

She said dressing like a man made me look dowdy and depressed and dull.

I said:

'I've just lost my lifelong lover of fifteen years, I don't think a shopping spree round 'What She Wants' is going to alter that do you?'

She said:

'Maybe not but at least it would help the Cause.'

I nearly smacked her legs.

She said:

'Dressing like a proper woman . . .'

Proper woman?

I said:

'Proper woman? What's a proper woman? Are women merely products of their clothes then?'

She said looking straight but announcing you're lesbian was confrontational to people, that it was politically subversive.

I said I didn't want to confront people thank you very much, I like to surround myself with like-minded friends.

(A subtle hint, but obviously too subtle because she insisted on persisting.)

She said it was a product of patriarchy that a lot of lesbians reject womanly images. Lesbians purport to love women but actually place male images in higher esteem and that it wasn't our fault but we were victims of a culture that strives to put women in second place and actually what we ought to be doing is revering images of femininity and reclaiming womanliness. She said there was an aggressive atmosphere on the lesbian scene that came from a mass dampening of the soft side of our psyche, that we were in effect unconsciously ashamed to be female.

This was when I hit her.

I said:

'I haven't spent forty-odd years being a dyed-in-the-wool dyke to have some wet behind the ears whippersnapper come along and spout ill-thought-out pseudo political psycho babble claptrap at me thank you very much, a man is a man and a woman is a woman, what they wear is irrelevant, it's how they behave that counts!'

Felt good at the time but I spent all night lying awake tossing and turning and worrying nonetheless. Oh, I can act tough, but underneath I hate hating, especially other lesbians – well, the scene's so small I might bump into her again.

We never had those kind of arguments when I first came to London.

We all looked the same when I came out – butch. Well, most of us, some femmes, but we didn't question and we certainly NEVER moralised.

Gateways was the place – it's closed down now, pity . . . but they've opened a chain of supermarkets in memory of it, touching I think, although I wouldn't buy the meat and dairy products there, not exactly renowned for high standards of hygiene.

And I'm on film. In *The Killing of Sister George*. In the Gateway scenes, in the crowd, that check shirt, it's mine – I think.

That's where I met Jackie in actual fact – Gateways. We were perfect for each other. Complemented each other perfectly. Agreed on everything, never argued, oh, sulked occasionally, both of us, but never really got fired up. Read the same books, liked the same TV programmes, had a small circle of friends that we could both stomach for more than a few hours, did a lot of home improvements and, thinking about it, I suppose we spent fifteen years slowly boring each other to death. And then of course there was the menopause.

Actually I've had one or two 'friends' suggest that to me about Sarah, which I think is a bloody cheek. Are you going out with a woman half your age because you're menopausal? No. I'm going out with a woman half my age because she's wonderful, she's fun, we have water fights and go to fairgrounds, and we don't care what we look like when we're dancing and she's not stuck in a rut and she coerces me to do things I've never tried before, and she laughs when I say I'm set in my ways and she tells me I'm a human being not a set course menu and for the last six months I've felt more like a human being than at any other time of my life – that's why I'm going out with a woman half my age.

Sarah. She took me to a drag club for my birthday, she did. I'd never been before, and I didn't want to go then. For one thing it was going to be full of men, she said, 'No, there'll be some women there,' but by the look on her face she meant possibly two at the most, and they'd probably be us, and I never particularly liked mixing with men. Nothing against them personally, it's just that I grew up being compared to them all the time, to such an extent that I came to resent them with a vengeance. They always seemed to have all the fun. Everything I wanted to wear, everything I wanted to do, everything I said, every move I made, 'What are you doing, Rose, trying to be a man?' No, I'm just trying to have fun. Arguing with Mother about going to some do or other, some special occasion. 'Wear a dress, Rose.' I don't like wearing dresses. 'You can't go in trousers, it's not done.' Well, I'm doing it. 'It's not ladylike.' I don't want to be a lady. 'Well, you can't be a man.' I don't want to be a man I just want to have fun! Of course I never did. If I lost I had to stand around frumped in a frock and if I won I had to stand around while everybody tutted and stared and muttered 'Penis Envy'.

Did I want a penis? No. Did I just want to have fun? Yes. What's the connection? I don't know but everybody else seemed to see one. Sarah says I was right all along otherwise they wouldn't have equated fun with having a penis, would they? Tell me now, Sarah, but where were you when I was fifteen, when I was spending all my formative years being made to feel somehow criminal, being made to feel that I actually did suffer from penis envy, that I hated men because I wanted to be a man, that I was denying my true gender, that I secretly hated being a woman, that I secretly hated all women – how can I hate women, I'm a lesbian! – Aha! that proves it's penis envy! ???? I wanted to run around, shout, let off steam, be horny and carefree and opinionated and drunk, I wanted to let my hair down, let my knickers down, go as I pleased, when I pleased, how I pleased, please myself, be selfish, be sexual, be myself. Was that having a penis? Apparently so. Be sensible. That was my lot. And I suppose for fifty-two years I have been just that – eminently sensible, afraid to have fun because 'What are you doing, Rose, trying to be a man?' Sarah, on the other hand, is brimming with confidence – gaily goes about doing whatever she wants and has two fingers firmly planted in the air when anybody questions her lifestyle.

She's beautiful. We met in a bookshop, she works there in fact. I don't usually even notice younger women, never mind lust after them, But Sarah bounced. Bounced and smiled and hummed and bounced. I hadn't had a decent relationship since Jackie left, let alone an indecent one, so I'd intended to buy one of those books that are written specifically for people to wallow in the tragedy of broken romance, a bit of dramatic misery helps pass the time I find. But Sarah, perhaps sensing my despair, perhaps being a cheeky little madam, said, 'How about a cook book?' and then promptly invited herself round for tea.

Six glorious months later and she's dragging me to a drag club for my birthday – and I mean dragging – I argued every step of the way. I said, 'The sort of men who do that are the sort who hate women.' She said, 'It's not like that.' I said, 'I don't like to see women all tarted up so why should I want to see men doing it.' She said, 'You'll be surprised.' I said, 'It degrades women, denigrates them, humiliates them, makes them objects of ridicule, figures of fun, it's downright mysogynistic, patriarchal, oppressive and thoroughly vulgar.' She said, 'Rose, if you are going to catch up with the colourful changes going on in the lesbian world then you're going to have to see clothes with a different eye.' I thought about colour and clothes and lesbians and decided she was bonkers and I did not want to go. Then we went inside.

Changed my life! It was like a burning bush on the road to Damascus! Hard to believe, I know. I used to think drag was a man putting on a dress and making lots of jokes about tits – not exactly world-shaking stuff. And try as I might I could not imagine Les Dawson as the new messiah – but that's because he's not, obviously. The Les Dawson School of Drag is simply men putting on a dress and making lots of jokes about tits. But this. This was something else. This was what I'd been looking for. This was fun.

Admittedly it was the boys who were having all the fun. A fact I resented with all my old venom – to begin with. Swishing and bobbing and bumping and grinding in their wigs and frocks and false eyelashes, showing off to a cheering and laughing crowd, strutting their stuff and saying to themselves: This is what I've wanted to do since God knows when, and people have said no, people have said, 'What are you doing, Roger, Bill, Ted, trying to be a woman?' And they've said, 'No, we're just trying to have fun.' I could hear it, I knew, I'd been there, been there all my life. We were the same, except they were finally having the fun – in public, on stage, to the hilt! I wanted to hit them, wanted to strangle them, because I wanted to do it too, I wanted to strut my stuff, I wanted to be myself, to the hilt, show everybody – This was what I wanted to do, this was my idea of fun. But in black? In trousers? Even a suit and tie, slicked-back hair and a dildo – not exactly showbusiness, is it?

But I knew what they were doing up there on that stage. Call it celebration, call it revenge, but the crowd loved them and the crowd accepted them and there's only one way to defy the people who tell you how to be – go public and get applauded.

Sarah laughs when I say I'm set in my ways and she tells me I'm a human being not a set course menu and for the last six months I've felt more like a human being than at any other time of my life – that's why I'm going out with a woman half my age. So I turned to her and I said, 'Sarah, get out your sequins we're going to revolt!'

Because did I ever at any time in my life want to be a man? No. So why dress like one? Because I didn't want to dress like a woman.

And, Mother, if you're up there watching, I hope you're proud.

Leaking From Every Orifice

Leaking From Every Orifice was written for and first presented at the 1993 Bisexual Conference, Nottingham, on 1 October 1993, and subsequently at the Battersea Arts Centre, London, on 22 March 1994.

Performed by Claire Dowie
Directed by Colin Watkeys

Part One

The sperm burrowed into my egg, the egg burrowed into my womb, the womb burrowed into the centre of my universe and I started singing 'I am woman hear me roar' and bursting into tears. What happened?

John Lennon happened. John Lennon and my first lesbian relationship.

About three years ago I was doing a show called *Why Is John Lennon Wearing A Skirt?*. Basically it was about how crap it is to be a woman. Took me two hours to explain that, now I can do it in a sentence. Should have done it then: 'Good evening, ladies and gentlemen, it's crap being a woman, thank you, good night.' That would've saved a lot of feminist discussion, wouldn't it? No it wouldn't. 'What do you mean by "crap"?' 'Whatever you want it to mean.' 'No I disagree, let's form a circle and discuss.' 'Okay fine.' Well, it would have saved a lot of life imitating art – well, not art exactly, a two-hour wank is more like it. Anyway, what it was really about was a tomboy growing into a woman and still being a tomboy because everything she feels is totally at odds with everything she's supposed to be as a woman (I said it was a wank). But the point is I mentioned motherhood, and I wasn't one, a mother, I mean, so this is where it all started. Or rather it all started with me mentioning motherhood in Birmingham. A fatal mistake – Birmingham. Birmingham is a fatal mistake, believe me, I come from there. Birmingham's so crap. In Birmingham when they built the National Exhibition Centre and discovered everybody was going to Manchester or London for the nightlife, Birmingham decided the best way to get them to stay was to provide more parking spaces. Birmingham decided to hold the Marlboro Grand Prix and then wanted to ban cigarette advertising. All Birmingham men have wispy moustaches and beer bellies, and all Birmingham men think they're good-looking. All Birmingham women wear white high heels and say, 'Wait for

me, Dave!' and think all Birmingham men are good-looking.
All Birmingham lesbians and gay men now live in London or
Manchester but park their cars in Birmingham.

Anyway, point is I did John Lennon in Birmingham and an
old school-friend was in the audience. In fact, she was my
best friend, my bestest ever friend – we spent from thirteen to
sixteen having sex in a broom cupboard, daily. Which is
where the expression 'Came out of the closet' comes from –
me. I started it, without knowing in fact. I didn't know
because at thirteen I'd never heard the word lesbian, let
alone what it meant, because in Birmingham there's only one
person at any one time who's gay, and they don't talk about
it, they just spend all their time packing their suitcase to
move to London or Manchester, and then when they've left
another gay person pops up, walks around Birmingham for a
bit, then starts packing. But I knew nothing about this at
thirteen, I was just happily fucking in a cupboard with my
best friend, while all the older pupils in my school were
walking past the cupboard hearing these strange noises,
looking in and next day presenting us with a suitcase – we
didn't know what it meant but we found if you used a lot of
lubrication it didn't half spice up our sex life. (Especially the
handle bit.)

So anyway, there she was, my bestest ever friend, about
twenty years later in the audience watching *John Lennon*. My
best friend. Okay, so she dumped me. That's all right, that
was twenty years ago. As soon as I finish the show I'm
rushing to see her. Okay, she dumped me for a bloke, no
problem, water under the bridge. I'm excited, I can't wait to
get to the bar. A bloke called Nigel. Nigel, I ask you, how can
you dump me for a bloke called Nigel? Doesn't exactly sound
racy, does he? Still, no matter, long time ago. I get to the bar
and kiss, kiss (because I'm theatrical now), and 'How are
you? Did you like the show?' 'No.' No? No? No.

She doesn't like my play. She doesn't think it's crap being a
woman, she likes being a woman. Why? Because she's a
mother now, and being a mother is (apparently) the most

important job in the universe, being a mother is akin to being in paradise, nirvana. A woman couldn't possibly fulfil her destiny in any other way than to be a mother. Oh, bleuch!

My best friend, my first lesbian relationship, I used to love this woman, I used to write her notes! And she's a mother now – not just any kind of mother, but one of THOSE kinds of mothers – all Early Learning Centre and face painting.

So what's so great about being a mother? Oh, I couldn't explain it (aha) it's a spiritual thing (ugh) but giving birth makes all those little patriarchal inconveniences just slip away into insignificance – I mean, let's be honest we know we can do anything a man can do, we don't need to prove it, but men can't nurture, can they? Men can't experience that deep bond between a mother and child – men will never know the joy and fulfilment of motherhood.

Oh yeah? Deep bond and fulfilment? So how much do you pay your childminder exactly?

Because if you've got friends who say, 'It's wonderful having kids' – just ask them how much they pay their nanny/childminder/au pair. If you've got friends who just go: ughhh (*Vacantly*.) – offer to baby-sit for an evening. Because it's shit having a baby, absolute shit.

So she starts talking about providing jobs for women and I'm bored with this conversation, I know that anything I'm going to say she's going to say, 'Well, you're not actually a mother yourself, so you don't know these things, do you?' So I go in search of a broom cupboard instead, just for old-times' sake – it works too, it seems everybody loves nostalgia, even fulfilled and joyful mothers. But at the back of my mind, even while we're lubricating the suitcases, a little voice is quietly saying:

Well, if you didn't like my show fine, can't please everyone, I mean, I'm not everybody's cup of tea, and I expect Nigel would have been funnier, but who knows, maybe next week, maybe next year, I'm going to get bloody even with you, you cow.

Didn't like my show. And that was it really, we exchanged phone numbers, but I didn't bother, we've really got nothing in common any more, and it's true what they say, you can never go back. So that was the end of that. Except:

Two years later I commit the cardinal sin, I have sex with a man – we thought we were being radical, political, because he was gay too. Turns out now, of course, we were at the forefront of queer, ahead of our time or what? (First time in my life I've been trendy.) Mind you, don't ask me what queer means because I'm damned if I know. I think it means that lesbians can now have sex with gay men, and vice versa. Funny I always called that straight myself. But there you go, have to move with the times.

But my God, it's hard being straight. I never realised before, there should be a song for it: Like 'Glad to be Gay', should be 'Hard to Be Het' or something. People should go on marches, have meetings about it. Because for one thing you don't understand what the other one is talking about. I've spent half the relationship with this man going, 'What?' And the other half going, 'Don't you get it?' And he keeps hanging around the flat. I keep thinking, 'What are you doing here? Can't you live in the shed or something?' And there's contraception to deal with. We have a choice because neither of us are HIV or anything and I don't want a choice, I know nothing about contraception. I'm supposed to be an intelligent thirty-five-year-old feminist woman and I go to the doctor's, she says, 'Well, what have you been doing all these years?' (Having fun mainly.) It's embarrassing. The only thing I know is that I don't want to go on the Pill. Not because I'm too old or because I smoke too much but because I can't bear the idea of spotting. Spotting – sounds disgusting, sounds like a dripping tap. 'Have you thought of using pantie liners?' Bugger off, I'm a lesbian – or at least I was. Pantie liners – we designed them curved because women are, fuck off. What do the other pantie liners do? Stick out like a plank? And what's this wings business – everybody knows, even men know, that if your knickers are tight you're okay, if your knickers are loose it's all going to fall down, wings and everything. Although a woman told me recently that wings aren't to keep the thing in place, it's actually to stop bits of blood seeping over the edges of your knickers. I just thought, 'Change more often, you slovenly bitch.' And wings make you chaff. They chaff you right here (*Between the legs.*), end up walking like John Wayne. Perhaps that's what they're for – pantie liners for dykes – 'Oh yes, I can spot and chaff at the same time, I'm tough me.' So. Don't want to go on the Pill.

What else is there? The cap. The cap's like half a tennis ball, well, without the fur, (at least mine doesn't have fur but then I wash mine a lot). Anyway, point is it bounces. You squeeze gunk all round it and bend it to put it in and it flies out of your hand and bounces round the bathroom, picking up bits of dirt and fluff and stuff and it always ends up in the toilet. (Told you I washed it.) Picking it out I think, 'Boy, do I feel horny now!' Meanwhile, he's in the bedroom putting on Shirley Bassey records – Gays can be so clichéd, can't they? I much prefer the originality of lesbians in construction helmets, and if they've got a spanner in their back pocket I'm gone! I'm spotting! So forget the cap. There's the IUD – well, I don't know about you but I don't want something that sounds like a terrorist organisation shoved up my uterus, using Semtex for lubricant, getting Radio Ireland every time I open my legs. So we've got condoms – dead balloons. Male condoms. Never tried those Femidom things, never been camping, wouldn't know how to put up a tent. So I say to my boyfriend, 'You put this dead balloon on your penis and then you put both penis and dead balloon inside me.' Okay? What could be simpler? Straightening the Leaning Tower of Pisa could be simpler. He knows nothing about women but has read articles about feminism (mostly in *Gay Times*) – he's sucking my toes and massaging my calves, I'm saying Higher! Higher! Stick it in me! Come on, you have my consent, come up, come up! He doesn't. He's worried about oppressing me with his penis. Oppressing me with his penis? Listen, pal, my vagina is going to have you surrounded, so how the hell can you oppress me? My vagina can surround

you, clamp on and suck your dick off your body in two
seconds flat should I desire it, because I've done the exercises
– you can do them at all times, girls, in the supermarket, at
the bus stop, in the hairdressers, the exercises are discreet,
feminine and odour free – and they enable you to fuck like a
rabbit, feel it and enjoy wave after wave of glorious orgasm –
and not only that but when you're pregnant you can cough
and not wet yourself.

So, I'm mixed up with a man, we have a discussion about
what he knows about feminism versus what I know about
being a woman and we finally fuck, and the condom breaks.

The condom broke, that's what happened. They don't make
condoms like they used to. Never had a condom break on me/
in me before. Mind you, I always slept with women, but
that's not the point, whatever happened to craftsmanship?

So my boyfriend starts panicking, he's running around the
flat finding spermicides, pesticides, insecticides, Coca Cola,
gin. Gin? Do you drink it or? . . . Whack it in! And I'm sitting
there giggling saying, 'I think I'll call it Jemima – how about
Elvis?' even while he's carrying me to the bathroom and
plonking me in a mustard bath.

Because this is a joke, right? I can't be a mother I'm only
fourteen and a boy – well, all right, maybe not, but it's an
ambition.

Mothers are all like Claire Rayner, they wear mother-type
dresses, like Claire Rayner, stay sober and are full of sensible
advice, like Claire Rayner: 'It's upsetting, luvvy, isn't it,
luvvy, you're upset, well, have a good cry and get yourself a
hobby'. So I'm just not the mother type – therefore it's not
going to happen, right? Wrong. Because he's panicking, he's
saying sensible things like, 'Go to the doctor and get the
morning-after Pill,' he even walks me down the next
morning, holding my hand like I'm seven. He doesn't laugh
at my jokes about Hoovers and knitting needles, he's taking
this seriously, he's behaving like an adult – so I might not be
the mother type, but he is, unfortunately he doesn't have the
necessary equipment, but I do. And doesn't this sound ever

so remarkably similar to what happened in *John Lennon*? . . .
Oh fuck.

So I get a home pregnancy kit, piss in a cup and put what
looks like a plastic lollipop stick in it – then we both stand
back and watch – (because it's a caring, sharing kind of
relationship). And then he gets an erection. He gets an
erection watching a lollipop stick turn pink. He gets turned
on by pink lollipop sticks – I don't do anything about it
because I'm a mother now, and mothers don't do that sort of
thing, mothers become incredibly practical and shuffle off to
the doctor's to give a blood sample and collect their baby
books, bursting into tears on the way. Why? Because it's your
hormones apparently, says so in the baby books, also tells
you to get a perm and wear make up to boost your morale, I
wonder if it's obligatory. I also wonder why you need your
morale boosting when everybody says I'm supposed to feel
fulfilled as a woman, it's supposed to be the most natural and
beautiful thing that's ever happened to me.

I come home to find my boyfriend still with an erection, still
staring at the pink lollipop stick – I'm surprised, I'd have
thought he'd have had a wank by now – I would've, except
that I'm a mother now and mothers don't do that sort of
thing. Well, they don't, let's be honest, can you imagine your
mother wanking your dad? No. Going down on him? Well, I
can't, I just know my mother doesn't do that sort of thing –
she's always been into fist-fucking for one thing.

So, I'm pregnant and terrified. I am going to be A Mother,
and you've got to pronounce it with a capital M. Why?
Because all the baby books and baby advertising and baby
shops and baby food manufacturers to. Patronising gits.
Mother, with a capital M. Like God with a capital G. You
are God, you are Mother, hear you roar, buy my stuff. The
condom breaks and suddenly I'm a deity, and I feel I can't be
all-powerful and all-knowing because they're trying to make
me feel guilty, they're trying to make me feel like a crap
mother because I can't make up my mind whether to use
Peaudouce or Pampers and already I'm two hours gone.

I don't want it. I can't take this pressure, I know fuck all
about babies and stuff. I mean, I've never seen one in my life
before. Well, I have, but I've crossed the road, that's the type
of person I am. I'm not the mother type, besides *John Lennon*
ended with an abortion so . . .

And then I start getting mystical, I don't want to, but I can't
figure it out. I don't believe in religion or anything but who
broke the condom? Why did the morning-after Pill not work,
or the spermicide – or anything? How did the condom break?
Why? It wasn't us, we put it on properly, were careful, used
proper lubrication, KY suits me. So who is this condom
vandal? Who's got it in for us? And then I figure it out. It was
God. Had to be because everybody goes on about this
benevolent father-figure but if you read His book He's a real
nasty piece of work. Smiting people and threatening to kill
Abraham's son and turning defenceless women into pillars of
salt just because she turned back wondering if she'd left the
gas on, and giving people boils and plagues and all manner of
nasty inconveniences. So of course it was God. He looks
down, sees us having fun and thinks 'Ha, look at them. They
think sex is for pleasure. I think I'll just bite their condom,
chew it up a bit,' (because God moves in very mysterious
ways). 'That'll bring them down to earth, turn them into
conservatives, toe the line, learn some depression. And
especially that female one, always arguing that motherhood
isn't necessarily fulfilling for all women – fuck her up, turn
her into a mother, let's see her argue then! Ha!' So it was
God. Had to be. The bastard.

And then I remember my first lesbian relationship. It all
makes sense. It was God. God broke the condom to help me
get even. I could defend my argument that it's crap being a
woman, by being a mother, going all the way that a woman
is supposed to go, and still finding it's crap, and then she'd
have to acknowledge it, my ex-girlfriend would have to
admit that my show was funny, interesting, true when you
think about it, and I'm infinitely better than Nigel and she
made a dreadful mistake dumping me – twenty years ago.

So I'm really into this, I'm about to become a born-for-the-first-time Christian Muslim Buddist Jew. But then my boyfriend interferes, picks up one of my baby books. And it doesn't even mention him. The book is distinctly called *Mother and Baby* book, Mother and Baby, Baby and Mother, doesn't mention him, doesn't mention 'sad old poof who can't get a boyfriend'. And he starts reading it and says, 'It's not God, look it says so, it's not God, it's your hormones. Your hormones can make you go a little bit irrational, emotional, mad.' He then ducks, because we've had this argument before, once a month in fact, if I wasn't hormonal when I was having periods, I am certainly not hormonal now that they've stopped.

I am immaculately pregnant. And I've decided to keep it because God wants me to get even with my ex-girlfriend. He also thinks Nigel's a bit of a wazzock too – He told me in a dream. I refuse to believe any garbage written in a baby book about hormones – I am not irrational, or emotional, everything seems perfectly reasonable to me. Like putting up shelves for instance . . .

As soon as I knew I was pregnant I had an overwhelming desire to put up shelves – no, that's not true – I had an overwhelming desire to get my 'man' to put up shelves for me. I wanted shelves everywhere. I wanted the whole flat covered in shelves. Why? Because you need shelves when you have children. It's obvious, you need shelves to put stuff on. You've got to have shelves to put stuff up high. Okay, I've got no stuff. I've got a flat full of empty shelves – but it's necessary, more necessary than eating coal anyway, especially since we've got no coal mines any more. I mean, blimey, that's irrational, that's hormonal: wanting coal when there's no coal mines. Perhaps I want shelves because B&Q is just up the road. I'm practical that way. Nothing irrational about me. And okay, so I'm crying at adverts. That's not my hormones, they're sad: 'We thought the garden was getting too much for you . . . (*Old man's look of alarm.*)' – that's sad! See, I'm not hormonal. Hormones are for cissy girls.

I'm not hormonal. But I am incredibly horny, I can't believe
how horny I am, I just want to have sex all the time. I think
this isn't like me so I have a look with a mirror – the whole of
my labia are permanently swollen, like when you've had
good sex and you can't pee properly, or one of those baboons
on heat that you see on the telly – they don't mention that in
the baby books. So I want sex all the time but I can't. Can't
have sex, can't even contemplate having sex till I've bought
myself one of those black, shiny, sexy, does up under the
crutch, all-in-one satiny things. I've got to have one. I don't
know why. I've never thought about those things before, big
knickers have always served me, but suddenly I've got to
have one, got to wear sexy stuff and because I'm pregnant I
even suddenly know where to get them – Marks & Spencer's!
(*Produces camisole thing from back pocket.*) So I buy one and of
course it doesn't fit, can't get it over my swollen breasts and
big belly, but that's okay, I just wear it around my neck, and
now I'm sexy. I can do anything now because I'm a sex
goddess and since we don't have to use condoms or anything,
we can fuck anywhere, anytime, and so long as I've got my
sexy round my neck, we do.

Except at antenatal classes. A real turn off. First thing they
asked was 'Who smokes?' (*Puts hand up, realises only one.*) I
thought they were going to pass them round and we'd all
light up and have a chat – turns out they wanted to let me
know I was killing my kid – hadn't even taken my coat off.
And they say mad things like 'Today we're going to teach
you to breathe.' Fuck off, I'm thirty-six I know how to
breathe, I've been doing it since I was two. But the maddest
thing of all, and what was mad was we all took it seriously,
was the time we passed round a breast pad so that we could
get used to it and we wouldn't be frightened of them when the
time came. Well, excuse me, but how many people do you
know are frightened of breast pads? How many people say
(*As though a spider.*) 'Oh my God, it's a breast pad!' How
many people even know what a breast pad is? I didn't. Till I
got pregnant I'd never heard of breast pads. Breast pads, if
you're wondering, are round pink things that you put over

your breasts to stop leakage. Because after you've had a baby, your breasts leak milk. At the most inconvenient times, they just go 'bleuch!' Like you get on a bus and the driver says 'where to?' and your breasts go 'bleuch!' So you get these huge dripping milk stains down your T-shirt unless of course you're wearing a breast pad, and then you just get nice round milk stains. It's more tidy and feminine we find. So we're passing round a breast pad and all the women are going 'Oh yes, I'm feeling calm with the breast pad, I'm taking the breast pad to me and I'm bonding with it, I am no longer afraid.' And then all the women pass it to their menfolk and all the men go (*As though a spider.*) 'Oh my God, it's a breast pad!' But the one thing they didn't mention at these antenatal classes, and it was the only reason I went, was: How do you become one of these mother things? How do you go from someone down here, to someone up there? How? And they didn't mention it, not once. And that's what's worrying me.

Then I wake up one morning totally paralysed (apart from my smoking arm obviously). Can't get out of bed. Tell my boyfriend I can't move because I don't know how to be a mother. He admits that he's terrified too, so we discuss for a while what would be good preparation for parenthood.

Sixty cigarettes later, he comes up with a brilliant idea: he says we should forget motherhood until it actually happens and instead revive *Why Is John Lennon Wearing A Skirt?* while eight months pregnant, because it would be funny, take our mind off things and it might earn us enough money to afford a cot. I then make a miraculous recovery and start beating him up, not because I'm hormonal or he's a gitty wanker with stupid ideas, but because, as it says in the baby books: 'It's harder for the man because he can feel left out whereas the woman just has to put up with discomfort and pain.' So of course I'm beating him up because God forbid he should be left out in the discomfort and pain department.

I then have a brilliant idea, I should forget motherhood until it actually happens and instead revive *Why Is John Lennon*

Wearing A Skirt? while eight months pregnant because that's where it all started, and it might give me some clues, and if I change the end from abortion to having it, going all the way that a woman is supposed to go, and then I invite my old lesbian girlfriend to sit in the front row and watch it – well, then it will all make sense, and she'll understand and fall on her knees apologising profusely for ever having dumped me for a wazzock like Nigel, and she'll offer to move in and help me raise it because she's a mother already and knows all about that stuff, and everything will be all right and wonderful.

So I then kiss my boyfriend's bruises better, have a fag and a shag and put up another shelf, happy in the knowledge that I'm finally going to get even with my ex-girlfriend and this pregnancy business will not have been for nothing.

Part Two

So I'm doing *Why Is John Lennon Wearing A Skirt?* while eight months pregnant. Unfortunately my old school-friend girlfriend didn't turn up – couldn't get a baby-sitter. Which was a drag because I'd rehearsed my argument with her more than I rehearsed the show. However, as it turned out it didn't matter because I loved doing *John Lennon* while eight months pregnant. Mainly to begin with because I thought throwing myself around the stage with such energy is bound to make me spontaneously combust – I think everybody else thought so too. Everybody was on standy-by, buckets and mops dotted around the stage in case my waters broke. Ambulances parked out front, a hot line to the hospital set up, earth-mother feminists thoughtfully brought their birthing pools with them, a doctor offered to check if my cervix was dilated in the interval . . . could have done with her during labour – but that comes later. But mainly people only bought tickets because they thought, 'Tonight's the night! Live on stage, life on stage – something creative in British Theatre – that's a first.' And nothing happened! And then I started thinking, 'If I can do this then being a woman is brilliant.' Look what I can do! I can do this (*Throws self around the stage.*) and I can do this! (*Hugely pregnant.*) Let me see a man do it! And if my lump is that tough she's gonna be the best bloody feminist in the whole world. She might be a big butch bull dyke on a motorbike! She might. Well, someone's got to have them, it could be me! I always knew she was going to be a girl – she had to be I wasn't having another male inside me – one was enough, and look at the trouble that caused!

So it's not crap being pregnant. Being pregnant is okay. What's crap is everybody else's response to it. 'Have a perm and wear make up to boost your morale.' Finding the writer of that garbage and stabbing them with a pitchfork would boost my morale.

Along with the people who tell you to take it easy, because
it's 'dangerous', you're in a fragile condition. 'We don't call
it an illness nowadays, but put your feet up, don't move and if
you feel a burst of energy – knit some bootees.' I had that
much energy I knitted a whole Wendy House. It was okay
though, it had gun turrets.

What's crap is complete strangers trying to make you feel
guilty for smoking. 'Do you know you're killing your child?'
'Wanna live long enough to find out, pal?'

What's crap is doctors, midwives and hospitals thinking
you've got nothing better to do in the whole world than to sit
waiting in a dirty, run-down cattle market with a lot of other
lumpy women, all of us clutching our urine samples for hours
on end, just so some gink in a white coat can say 'you're
healthy'. I know. 'You should stop smoking.' I know. 'Had a
perm yet?' No.

And you're the lucky one because at least you've finally been
seen. 'Excuse me, I've been waiting for four hours and I've
run out of things to eat.' 'The doctor's having his lunch at the
moment, can you come back tomorrow?' 'I've got a very
important meeting tomorrow.' 'More important than your
child?'

Mind you, it's not all a waste of time at these hospital places,
at least while you're waiting you can learn your list of
euphemisms: privates, front bottom, back bottom, down
there, waterworks, plumbing, female parts, female things,
down below, nether regions, downstairs department, bottom
bits, underside. 'Excuse me, I just want to have a poke
around your feminine mystique.' You what? Do you mean
my vagina?

But what's most crap is the thought that at the end of these
glorious nine months (or rather ten months – another thing
they get you with, forty weeks is ten months – these shit bag
baby people can't even do maths), but the thing that's most
crap is the thought that at the end of these glorious, lumpy,
energetic, sexy ten months I'm going to have to deal with the

end of life as we know it – if you could ignore that, pregnancy would be great.

And don't even talk to me about labour. Don't even mention it!

As soon as the contractions started, I started becoming woman, at one with nature, giving birth to the mother inside me, becoming whole, finding the goddess within me, fulfilling my potential, becoming a real woman, becoming 'She'. I thought 'Yes, this is it, this is real, I'm going to grow herbs and bake bread . . . oh, I can't really explain it, it's a spiritual thing . . .' Then it all went horribly wrong – thank God.

As soon as the midwife turns up you've got a husband – Hello, hubby – excuse me, when did that happen? When did I get married? Where's all the presents? And another list of euphemisms to learn: mum, mother, dearie, darling, sweetheart, luvvy and, from an eighteen-year-old whippersnapper student midwife, 'Chickie!'

Chickie? Chickie? I'm a thirty-six-year-old human being, am I about to lay an egg? And she's stroking my hand – stop stroking my hand! I used to be tough, I used to be one of THOSE kind of feminists – you know, Frightening – with a capital F – now I am approaching motherhood I am becoming at one with the great goddess woman and if she doesn't stop stroking my hand I'm going to beat the shit out of her. Chickie. 'Do you feel a contraction, chickie? Would you like some water, chickie?' Would you like to stop ruining my birthing experience sister?!

It was great actually, it was wonderful, so sexual, like one long sex session, lasting hours. They don't mention that in the baby books. Mainly, it was me and my 'man'. The midwives kept out of it to begin with, so that me and my 'husband' could 'bond' – worst of it was we bloody did! Leaning on him to contract, holding onto his belt loops, the two of us together, entwined in this sensual, sexual journey to birth. 'Do you want to get naked too?' 'No thanks, I've got an erection' 'Okay'. As I felt the contraction roll through my body, it passed to his and he rolled with me, and we moved and breathed together and at one point I looked at him and I thought, 'God, I love this man, I really do,' then I thought, 'I'm gasping for a fag' so snuck into the dogs' room to smoke and bond with them for a bit. Midwives are funny about dogs – they don't mind you having them, they'd just prefer you kept them in another room while giving birth – can't think why? They're my children from my lesbian days.

I was having a home birth by the way, you probably realised that otherwise you'd wonder what the NHS was coming to: giving birth in one room with a vet's next door. It's funny, as soon as you mention home births all the midwives immediately think you're into aromatherapy, beanbags and dolphin music – I just wanted a home birth so I could smoke. I was so terrified of not being allowed to smoke I thought I'm staying at home with lots of ashtrays around me. The midwife said it's the first time she'd interrupted labour for a fag break, I said, 'Yeah, me too.'

And then I don't know what happened. I think the midwives must have got a bit bored because next thing I know they're manually breaking my waters and telling me to push. And then I'm on all fours, sweaty and sticky and throwing up and pushing God knows what, I don't, out the other end, certainly not a bundle of joy anyway, face all puffy, hair plastered in sweat to me head, looking completely wrecked and exhausted and he says, 'God, you're beautiful!'

Now this is weird, because I suddenly had this incredible flash. I shouted, 'Stop the contractions I want to discuss!' Because it suddenly occurred to me – sex. Men and sex. What's that all about? Are men interested in women? Real women? I mean, it doesn't exactly come naturally to them, does it? Maybe I'm wrong but there seems to be two types of women that men go for: women who are like one of the boys – in which case you might as well go for one of the boys, stop pretending – I've got that sort – or women who have gone to extraordinary lengths to disguise themselves. I reckon if a woman laid out all her man-catching stuff on the bed –

painted the make up on the duvet, like a duvet face – put a
woman's wig and earrings and jewellery – then the flouncy
blouse, skirt, stockings, high heels, all stuff like that –
plumped the duvet to make it look like it's been on a diet,
shaved all the fluffy bits and dog hairs off, and then waited,
stood back as a natural woman, naked, eating – I bet the
man would fuck the duvet.

Because I don't think men are attracted to women. I think
men have to be trained into being attracted to women.
Which is why we're constantly bombarded with images of
women. Like – keep the man in custody long enough and
eventually he'll confess – bombard men with images of
women long enough and eventually he'll fuck. It's a species
survival conspiracy. Take the Cadbury's Flake ad as an
example – we all think it's the sexy woman selling the Flake –
wrong. It's actually the Flake selling the sexy woman.
Because men have no problem wanting a Flake, they like
Flakes, it's the woman we've got to sell him. Same with
women and cars: men love cars, they want cars – put a
woman next to the car and eventually, hopefully, he'll want
a woman. It works too. This is why men are obsessed with
women: because everything they've ever wanted, from a bag
of nails to a BMW, there's always a woman attached. Girlie
magazines are the supreme achievement of the species
conspiracy. A man wants a wank. He doesn't know how to,
because men are like that. He needs to buy a magazine, like
What Car? magazine. He buys *What Wank?* magazine – full of
women – so it finally clicks. He thinks, 'Oh, that's what
they're for, I get it now.' Really, if he was left alone and we
didn't bother with all this sexy lady stuff bombarding his
brain space, he'd just go trainspotting and be happy.

Everybody knows this deep down. Everybody knows that it's
really women who are the sexual creatures. That's why
women's sexuality has been bumped down and men's
bumped up, so that they can meet in the middle, otherwise
men would be saying, 'Not again, not again!' It's been going
on for centuries, since Adam and Eve, the first man and
woman on earth – apparently. Eve says, 'Fancy a fuck,

Adam?' He says, 'Nah, I'm busy looking at these trees, I'm doing something important.' So Eve gets an apple. 'Fancy an apple, Adam? Eh, Adam? . . .' (*Waves it around getting nearer and nearer the groin.*) Because Mars Bars weren't invented in those days.

Then I suddenly realise I'm not in the place I thought I was. I'm lying on my bed sucking in all this gas and air. I'm in the middle of labour. I've got an overwhelming urge to push but everybody's screaming at me not to. I don't know what's happening. They keep trying to explain to me that my cervix wasn't fully dilated and the pushing has swollen it up so the baby can't get out – I keep saying, 'Yeah, yeah, but what do you think about men and sex? Do you think it's natural?' My boyfriend concludes that I'm allergic to gas and air and he wants to beat up the midwives for breaking my waters and telling me to push in the first place, they're screaming, he's swearing and I'm burbling 'Give Nigel a Flake!' – it's all incredibly spiritual.

Everything went wrong. I was really out of it, completely doped up with this gas and air. Till the ambulance people arrived – 'Oh, wow, dykes! Take me to Birmingham Accident and tell me about yourselves. Are you doing anything tonight? What this old thing? Oh, no, just a spot of man trouble, I can handle it, now, about your uniforms . . .!'

Unfortunately they dumped me at the nearest hospital. I tried explaining I wasn't looking my best but they wouldn't listen. So, they stick me in this room for sixteen hours, all decorated in Laura Ashley, to make me feel at home. Well, I'm sorry but a mountain of washing up, stuff and junk piled everywhere, the TV blaring and lots of ashtrays would make me feel at home. Laura Ashley? No. And there's lots of machinery and they're sticking something in my back to make me go numb from the waist down. It's a different set of midwives except for the whippersnapper student, she's staying for support and she's still stroking my hand! I'm so gaga I'm beginning to fancy her. Then it gets serious. It must be serious because they take me out of the Laura Ashley and dump me in the butcher's next door. There's a big slab and they slap me on it, shave all my pubic hair, stick my feet in stirrups and tell me to push. Push what? I'm completely paralysed from the waist down, all I can see is two lardy legs stuck up in a very unfeminine fashion, and I'm thinking they could have shaved my legs while they were at it, looks stupid otherwise, no wonder the ambulance crew didn't fancy me. They tell me to pretend to push. I'm crap at acting so since my belly button is the last thing I can feel I try pushing that out instead – told you I was gaga. Then suddenly, with the help of a pair of forceps, I go from a womb to a tit at the stroke of a contraction.

So far motherhood sucks. Literally.

But at least I discover that there is actually a smoking room in hospital. I didn't have to ask, I just followed my nose, which was useful because you couldn't see anything for the fug. The whole of two labour wards were crammed into this tiny broom cupboard – brought back strange sexual memories for me – kept asking if anybody had bought suitcases.

So I spend a day in hospital trying to find out how to become a mother, because I still feel like myself and nothing's changed. They tell me I can go home once I've learnt how to bath the baby. Apparently this is all you need to know about babies, how to bath them. An orderly shows me how it's done. She picks my baby up and straight away it starts screaming. Screams all the way through the bath – I think yeah easy, I can do that, I can make a baby cry – in fact I could do it without water, just pinch it. So then I can go home, well, after a slight tussle – the nurse chasing me down the corridor with the baby yelling, 'You're supposed to take it with you!' I'm yelling, 'Toss off, I've done my bit, I only came in for liposuction.' I still don't know about motherhood.

And then off we all go home, with my boyfriend driving at five miles an hour with his hazard warning lights on.

A friend of ours who still thinks of me as lesbian and my boyfriend as gay reckons it's the most miraculous birth since Jesus Christ – we're affronted – she is Jesus Christ. The new Jesus is going to be a big butch bull dyke on a motorbike, and one day she's going to grow up and save the world! We keep having to say that because that's the only reason we can think of to keep her, I mean, she doesn't do anything! We've tried throwing sticks but she won't fetch them. So that's our reason, she's going to be the new messiah. Better than other reasons I've heard:

Well, we had a baby to keep our marriage together – How? Are they hoping it'll grow up quick and become a counsellor for Relate? Or maybe it'll be useful to pass the crockery for you to throw at each other. And I don't know who these people are who say couples should stay together for the sake of the kids, they're probably single and child-free because in my experience, nine months' worth, it's the kids that break the couples up. We used to be best friends but now we spend our whole life working in shifts. He works while I look after her. Then I work while he looks after her. We don't see each other at all except to argue because he thinks he's doing more than I am and I think he's doing more than I am, but I'm not going to tell him. And it's hideous – you both grow to hate and resent each other, with time only to argue – usually in note form.

But it's not all bad, it's given me an insight into why gays are given such a hard time: jealousy. People are jealous of lesbians and gays because they're least likely to accidentally have children.

Mainly it seems most people have children because it just happens. Apparently eighty per cent of pregnancies are 'accidental'. The other twenty per cent are by people rich enough to afford nannies/childminders/au pairs and later on, boarding schools. There's only twenty per cent of the population controlling their destiny. The other eighty per cent are standing around saying, 'What the fuck happened? Do you suppose it was God then?' 'I don't know but I'm going to find a gay person to hit.' 'What's it got to do with them?' 'Nothing but they're gay and smug and happy and I hate them.'

Because it's horrible, you're just damp all the time. Damp. 'By the way, how are you, down there, you know, your undersides?' Still leaking thank you. 'Any baby blues?' You get this thing called the baby blues – 'After about four days you may experience the baby blues' – they don't tell you when it's going to stop though. You just stand there and all of a sudden . . . (*Starts crying, then leaking from vagina, then leaking from breasts.*) . . . And that's just the men.

Went to the antenatal class reunion, that was good. That's when everybody has had their babies and gets back together again. Everybody going, 'Let me see yours, oh, cute (not as nice as mine).' Then we all sat down to complain about how crap it all was – everybody had a horror story – and the one who had the most to complain about, of course, was the one man who turned up – what a git – the trauma of having to watch, poor lamb – 'and there was nothing I could do, I had to stand there while she suffered it was horrible, I just felt so helpless and . . . and . . . this doctor came with these big scissors and cut her vagina and her vagina went phlat! – it was awful . . .' So we all clucked like broody hens – or should that be chickies? – gave him some hot sweet tea for the shock . . . Yes I know, I never should have taken him, but he's more of a mother than me. Then the midwife who was running the show (and had had kids) said, 'So how do you all feel now?' We all sat in a circle smiling, and I'm thinking, 'Here we go – we all feel fulfilled and beautiful and happy and blah blah blah.' Till one women piped up with, 'Well, actually I feel a bit trapped.' Then another woman said, 'Yes, so do I.' Then they all started: . . . 'God, isn't it awful? . . . I feel like my previous personality has been blown out of the window and I'm left with just this constant crapness' . . . 'Yeah, I keep waking up and the baby's still there!' . . . 'And it's going to be till it's eighteen!' . . . 'Or older!' . . . 'I was an intelligent person, now my life seems to solely consist of me saying Will you please just fart!' . . . 'Why did nobody tell us it was going to be so crap!' And I'm thinking, 'No, it can't be crap, we can't all think it's crap, not all of us, one or two yeah, but not everybody. If we just think about it, just click it round, look at it from a different perspective, because it's natural after all, we've just got to click, think about how it could be, see it from a different angle, just click a little, click . . . it could be . . . could be . . .' No. Motherhood's crap.

It is, it's a myth. This idea that a woman's fulfilled, people just hear her wrong, they say, 'How is it?' and she says, 'I'm full. Filled. Had it up to here, can't take any more!' It is, all of it, crap, the responsibility, the pressure, the feeling of being trapped, unable to move. I've spent the last nine months going Ughhh. (*Vacantly.*) No, that's not true, there's one thing about it that's not crap, and that's what makes it really annoying. Because the baby's not crap. The baby's beautiful, wonderful and that is so annoying, because if the baby was crap I could just throw her in the dustbin and everything would be all right. But everything else. Can't go out, can't go anywhere, can't even go to the pub for five minutes. I used to like going to the pub for five minutes. I used to like going to the pub all day. Now you can only have dinner parties with other people who are embroiled in the crapness and it's not nice because you can't eat proper food. You have to eat Brie and drink wine and talk about schools and nurseries and growth spurts as though it's interesting and it's horrible, horrible, horrible!

And then I remember my first lesbian relationship – the reason I'm where I am now. Of course – I can finally get even – I can finally win! I phone her. I say, 'Motherhood's crap!' She says, 'Yes, I know.' 'Well, why didn't you tell me?' 'Because you were gay and smug and I hated you and I wanted to get even.' Then she says, 'Oh, by the way, remember Nigel?' 'Nigel? Vaguely.' 'Well, he had an operation, he's a woman now. But unfortunately he'll never be able to have children.' 'Oh.' Right. Fine. Bloody Nigel – wait till I get even with him!